To Dear Daniel with Love…

The life and times of a Walthamstow girl

By

Mo Ann Shanks

Published by New Generation Publishing in 2015

Copyright © Maureen Shanks 2015

First Edition

The author asserts the moral right under the Copyright, Designs and Patents Act 1988 to be identified as the author of this work.

All Rights reserved. No part of this publication may be reproduced, stored in a retrieval system or transmitted, in any form or by any means without the prior consent of the author, nor be otherwise circulated in any form of binding or cover other than that which it is published and without a similar condition being imposed on the subsequent purchaser.

www.newgeneration-publishing.com

ACKNOWLEDGEMENTS

I would like to thank my dear Husband Roy for all his patience and encouragement whilst I have been ensconced in my office typing away on the computer.

My sincere thanks also goes to my best friend Marion Cunningham who as a published Author herself has given me invaluable advice, support and encouragement without which I don't think I would have ever completed the task of writing these my memoirs.

Thanks must also go to all family and friends who are depicted in the book and a special thanks to Bill Bayliss for allowing me to use a sketch of Priory Court as one of the illustrations. A special mention goes to the Curator of the Vestry House Museum who was very helpful and permitted me to scroll through the archives of old photographs until I found an early photo of Priory Court where I lived from 1949 until my wedding in 1961.

My thanks and gratitude goes to Mandi Spink who gave me permissions to use the photo of our grandson Daniel for the front cover of my book. The photograph was taken at Mandi's wedding in 2005 when Daniel was just 3 years old.

Last but not least my beloved grandson Daniel who gave me inspiration to write my memoirs in the first place.

Author's Note

This book is a biography following my childhood years growing up in Walthamstow East London during the Second World War and post-war years.

I was inspired to write down and record these memories by my young Grandson Daniel when he would ask me to tell him stories about my childhood - hence the title 'To dear Daniel with love...'

When I made the decision to write these stories I didn't realise what a marathon task it would turn out to be. As my fingers flew over the keyboard memories came flooding back. In 1949 my family moved from Erskine Road Walthamstow to Priory Court which was a new Council Estate where I spent my teenage years. Then my friend and I got chatting to a group of boys and a nice young man called Roy caught my eye and 4½ years later we were married.

I have enjoyed every moment writing these stories and I very much hope they will be enjoyed not only by my family but also anyone who remembers Walthamstow in the old days.

In loving memory of

William Albert (Bill) Betts
1925 – 2014
And
Leonard (Lenny) David Betts
1933 - 2015

4

CHAPTER ONE

My Father's Family.

My story begins with the most important people in my life, my parents Tom and Ivy Penn. I tell how they first met and of course I introduce both sets of grandparents who featured greatly in my early years.

My father was born in Mile End Old Town – now known as Stepney - to Charles Edward George Penn and his wife Mary Elizabeth Penn (nee Jeapes) on 06 July 1913 He was called Charles Alfred after his father but both Charles Senior and Charles Junior were known by the nickname 'Tom'– I have never discovered the reason why. So for the purpose of this story we will call him Tom.

Dad was the third child and the eldest son – three more sons were born to my grandparents after Dad.

They lived at number 12 Ernest Street and it would seem that over a period of time various members of the family had resided at different addresses in the same street.

My father left school at 14 having gained his Matriculation – which is similar to the school exams taken today. He was a bright boy so his father apprenticed him to a Carpentry and Joinery firm specialising in building shop fronts. He attended 'Night School' to gain his qualifications and he enjoyed his work.

My granddad worked in a sea-sponge Factory as a sponge cutter which was a skilled job, one slip of the knife and the sponge would be ruined. The sponges would be delivered into the factory where they were cleaned and it was my granddad's job to cut them into various sizes. I believe he also worked as a Journeyman as it was known in those days which meant he was apprenticed to a trade.

Granddad Penn circa 1920

Granddad Penn Sergeant in the Army in the First World War

Granddad enlisted in the Army on the 15th May 1916 and was placed on a Reserve list as he was a married man. He was then called up on 3 March 1917 and was seconded to the Royal West Surrey Regiment where he showed leadership qualities and on 09 July 1918 he was promoted to the rank of Sergeant. During his time in the Army he was sent to France where he was unfortunate to become a victim of mustard gas. He was evacuated to England on a hospital ship the HMS St. Patrick suffering from Bronchial Pneumonia and chronic Bronchitis He was demobbed in March 1920.

My granddad was a good old East Ender born and bred and he loved nothing better than to take his brood of children in a Pony and Trap all around London visiting the famous sites. The children looked forward to these outings very much. Although granddad was quite strict I believe he loved his children very much but in those days it was 'not the thing' to show emotion.

My Mother's family

Mum was one of 9 children; but unfortunately her older brother John died on the 14 January 1918 at the age of 2 years and 9 months from tuberculosis, peritonitis and measles, therefore my mother became the eldest child. She was born on 05 July 1916 to John Thomas Betts and his wife Ivy Annie Betts (nee Ward) – my mother was also called Ivy Annie. They lived at number 18 Pollard Street Bethnal Green. My grandparents then went on to have a further seven children as large families were the norm in those days.

Mum had suffered ill health from an early age so her schooling was sporadic and she had to attend what was termed 'a special school'. A bus would collect her every day to take her to her special school. It must have been upsetting not being able to go to school with her siblings. She was often ill and suffered with a heart condition and also a nervous disease called St. Vitus Dance. During these periods of ill health she would be hospitalized and on one occasion she was taken to a hospital in Kent which made it very difficult for her parents to visit her.

In spite of her illnesses she was clever with a needle and enjoyed knitting. Nan had been a Seamstress before she married so no doubt mum inherited her skills with the needle.

As there was never much money coming in – granddad, who was a cobbler by trade, was amongst those who were out of work during the great depression in the 1920s and 1930s. So mum learned how to make her own clothes and she would earn extra money by visiting the local Jewish homes on Saturdays which was their Sabbath, lighting their fires and carrying out general chores. Their religion forbade then to undertake any of these tasks on that day.

Having spoken to my remaining aunties they told me that they were all expected to do their bit to bring money into the household. Aunties Violet, Pat and Rose also had to visit the Jewish households to light their fires and carry out menial tasks or do the shopping.

Granddad did his bit by mending shoes for the local neighbours. He would send the children to the local Leather shop with the money and a note as to what kind of leather to buy for the shoes that he happened to be mending at the time. It had to be the right one, thick leather for men's shoes and thinner leather for the ladies. Woe betide if one of the children came back with the wrong leather, they were promptly despatched back to the leather shop to get the right one. He would sit at his cobblers' lasts after shaping the leather and fixing it in place on the sole of the shoes with the tiny tacks which he kept in his mouth. Unfortunately this habit had the effect of turning his teeth black over the years.

Granddad also worked in Spitalfields market which dealt with fruit and vegetables. His job was to take the empty crates back to the wholesalers. To enable him to carry as many of the crates as he could he would have to place a flat leather cap upon his head on which he could balance the crates.

My uncles also had their part to play in the family finances. They would visit Spitalfields market at the end of the day and grab any old crates that were lying about. These would be swiftly chopped up and sold as firewood to mainly to the Jewish community or anyone else who would buy the kindling. Sometimes they had collected so much firewood that they found it difficult to carry so they would wait for a passing lorry and cheekily grab a lift on the back, more often than not they would be caught and told to 'clear off you little blighters'.

Nanny Betts as a young woman of about 18 years old

Nanny Betts with Johnny aged 2 and mum as a baby on Nan's lap.

Mum and Dad's Courtship

The following story was told to me by my mum when we would sit together and she would reminisce about her past life.

Ivy left school at 14 years old and went to work as a machinist in a factory. She had made a few friends but one special friend was a girl called June who was about a year older. One day June asked Ivy if she would like to accompany her to a dance that was being held at the local Town Hall that Saturday, Ivy said she would like to go but would have to check with her parents to see if it was ok.

The family were all sitting around the table eating their meal that evening when Ivy broached the subject of the dance to her parents. Nanny Betts was definitely the authoritarian in the family whilst granddad, well was granddad, he was a quiet man and went along with anything that his wife said. So it was to her mother to whom Ivy addressed the question and told her about the dance and asked permission to go. Her mother pondered on this for a while but realising that her daughter was now growing up and earning her own money she agreed to let her go. Then Ivy suddenly realised that she didn't have anything nice to wear. All her clothes were just serviceable working clothes. She mentioned this to her mother and that she hadn't time to look around the shops to buy something. Her mother, ever the resourceful woman thought for a moment then said that she had to go into the market the next day and she knew where there was a stall which sold some nice material and whilst in the market said that she would pick up a dress pattern. Then between them they could make a dress in time using her mother's old sewing machine. That pleased Ivy no end.

The next day when Ivy went into work she excitedly told her friend June that she would love to go to the dance with her. That night when she arrived home from work Ivy's mother called her into the parlour and there on the table was a brown paper parcel. Ivy eagerly tore the paper open and there inside was a length of lovely blue material with tiny white daisies all over it. Her mother had also thoughtfully purchased some little pearl buttons which she suggested could be sewn down the front of the dress which would finish it off nicely. She added that there would probably be enough material to even make a belt to match which would go around the waist and tie up at the back.

Then delving further into the package, Ivy brought out the dress pattern. It was very pretty with a sweetheart neckline and short puffed sleeves, and nipped in at the waist. It had a full skirt which ended fashionably just below the knee.

After everyone had eaten and the china and cutlery had been put away, Ivy and her mother retired into the drawing room where the sewing machine had already been set up. Together they laid the pattern on the material and carefully cut around it. Ivy then set about tacking all the pieces together ready to be machined the next day.

As soon as she got home from work the next evening Ivy couldn't wait to start on the dress. She managed to sew most of the dress together when her mother came in and told her it was late and she should be getting to bed, but she promised Ivy that when she had finished her chores the next day she would finish the dress for her.

True to her word when Ivy arrived home from work that evening, the dress was almost finished. All that remained to do to complete the task was to stitch the pearl buttons down the front. Ivy tried the dress on and it fitted perfectly. She thought that the black patent shoes which she kept for best would go nicely. Her mother had thought of everything and as a surprise she produced a small black evening bag which completed the ensemble. She had seen this on a second hand stall whilst visiting the market and had haggled with the stall holder and bought it quite cheaply.

Saturday arrived and Ivy carried out her usual chores visiting the local Jewish homes and lighting all their fires and also making trips to the shops to carry our errands for the ladies of the house. She had earned some extra money to spend that evening and to repay her mother for the dress material.

She had arranged to meet June at the bus stop to catch the 7 o clock Ivy's mother was very strict and as Ivy was going out of the door she warned her to be home by 10.30 as the last bus left at 9.45.

They arrived at the town centre and alighted from the bus and walked across the road to the Town Hall, entering the large wooden doors they paid their entry fee at the kiosk then carried on to the hall itself via the glass swing doors. At the end of the hall there was a stage on which the musicians were tuning their instruments. Chairs and small tables had been placed on either side of the hall which was filling up quite quickly. Ivy and June made their way over to a group of their friends from the factory where two seats had been saved them.

There was a refreshment bar at the opposite end of the hall where they sold non-alcoholic drinks and snacks. June asked Ivy if she would like a drink and she replied that she would like an orange juice, so whilst she sat down and chatted to their other friends, June went over to the bar to get their drinks.

Ivy had never been in this hall before and she was taking in the sights. Above the hall in the ceiling was a large round crystal ball and as it gently turned it threw prisms of light all around the hall which bounced off the walls like so many rainbow stars.

The band began to play and couples were getting up to dance. A couple of lads who had been standing near to the girls, walked over to them. One was dark haired and wore glasses and the other had fair hair. The dark haired lad asked June to dance and the fair haired lad came over to Ivy. "Would you like to dance love?" he asked, Ivy said she would, although she wasn't very good at dancing having not had a lot of practice and she felt quite awkward. However they got chatting and she soon relaxed. The lad told her his name was Tom Penn, he was 18 years old and that he was an apprentice Shop fitter from Mile End Old Town. She in turn told him her name and that she was 15 years old and lived in Bethnal Green and worked in the local dress factory as a machinist.

During the evening Tom claimed most of the dances with her and all too soon it was time to leave. Ivy motioned to June who was enjoying herself dancing with various boys. She was quite a popular girl and very outgoing compared to Ivy who tended to be quite shy until she got to know people. "Come on June we had better go now if we are to get the last bus". So they put on their coats and then said their goodbyes to their friends and the lads who had joined them. Tom then took hold of Ivy's arm and said he would walk her and June to the bus stop. She thought that was very nice of him. Then Tom's friend Reg came over and joined them and together the four of them left the hall with Reg holding June's arm. Tom and Ivy chatted away and he asked if he could see her again. He said that there was another dance next week and he would love it if she could come. Ivy said she would love to. They didn't have to wait long before the bus arrived so saying goodbye to the two lads June and mum got on and sat down.

On the way home Ivy thanked June for asking her to go to the dance with her and said she had had a lovely time. She then excitedly told June that Tom had asked her out again the following Saturday. June replied that Reg had also asked her out again so the two girls decided that they would be at the dance next Saturday.

When Ivy arrived home her mother was waiting up for her and wanted to know how the evening had gone. Ivy told her about meeting with the young man called Tom and that he had asked her out the next week. Her mother was pleased that she had met someone, but warned her to be careful, but didn't enlighten her as to what she meant. Her mother was quite old-fashioned in that she had never discussed sex with any of her daughters nor did she really explain about periods or having babies suffice to say that when Ivy or her sisters did start their periods, all she would say was "Don't go near any boys". Perhaps she should have followed her own advice, as I found out after she had passed away that she had been 8 months pregnant with John when she married.

So Ivy and Tom continued to see each other over the ensuing months, until one day her mother suggested that it was about time that she brought this young man home to meet the family. "Why don't you bring him round to tea next Sunday?" she said. Ivy met Tom as usual that evening and passed on her mother's invitation which Tom accepted.

Ivy had warned her younger brothers and sisters to be on their best behaviour as she didn't want them to embarrass her in front of Tom.

Sunday arrived and Ivy helped her mother with the tea, there were homemade cakes and fish paste sandwiches her mother had laid on a really nice spread.

There was a knock on the door and Ivy went to open it and Tom stood on the doorstep. He wore a check jacket over a white shirt with a yellow tie; a mustard coloured waistcoat and a pair of beige trousers which had been pressed to perfection with sharp creases down each leg. On his feet were highly polished brown shoes. He explained to Ivy much later that because his father had been in the army he was a stickler for smartness and had instilled this in his son.

He made a very good impression on Ivy's parents and they liked him straight away. Even her younger brothers and sisters were all on their best behaviour which of course, pleased her.

After that first visit Tom was a regular visitor to the Betts household. Then Tom took Ivy to meet his family who had invited her to tea at their house in Ernest Street. She got on well with his parents, his brothers and two sisters.

The house in which Tom's family resided was a large four-storey building. His family occupied the two floors whilst another family occupied the other part of the house.

Tom's mother Mary was a tiny woman; around 4ft 10" tall, very slim with dark hair which she wore rolled into a curl around her head and on top of this she wore a hair net to keep it in place. She had pale blue eyes and wore plain wire framed glasses. Her friendly smile soon put Ivy at ease, and before long they were chatting away as if they had known each other all their lives.

Tom senior, in complete contrast to Mary, was a tall man around 5ft 10" with a big bristling moustache which made him look a bit fearsome at first sight. Because he had been a Sergeant during the First World War he possessed a rather loud booming voice which was a bit frightening but Ivy soon became accustomed to this and quite liked him. He always wore a flat cap on his head as was normal apparel for men in those days.

Ivy was introduced to Jinny and Hetty, Tom's two elder sisters. Jinny was unmarried but Hetty was engaged to Arthur Miles and they were planning to get married in two years' time. To complete the family were Tom's 3 younger brothers, Bill, who at 16 was 2 years younger than Tom, Alf and Ted. Alf had just left school and was embarking on his career but Ted was still a schoolboy.

It was early 1933 and Ivy had just got home from work and her mother was making tea as usual. Ivy looked at her mother and thought to herself '*Is it my imagination or is mum putting on weight*', she just put it down to her age, and thought no more about it. After they had cleared the tea things away Ivy went to get ready to meet Tom and her mother took her to one side and said "Ivy I've got something to tell you" Ivy looked worried wondering what it could be. Then her mother announced that she was going to have another baby. Ivy couldn't believe what she was hearing; surely her mother was too old to still be having children. In actual fact she was 40 years old but I suppose it seemed old to Ivy at that time when she herself was only 17 years old. She didn't say anything as her mother went on "The baby is due around June time". Ivy was shocked and without thinking she said "Aren't you a bit old to be having another baby?" to which her mother replied "Well it's not as if it was planned these things happen, but being the eldest I just wanted to let you know".

Ivy then left and went to get ready to meet Tom. They had planned to go to the local cinema and all through the picture she was very quiet and hardly spoke. In the end Tom asked her what was wrong. She burst into tears and said "Mum told me tonight that she is expecting another baby in June isn't that disgusting?" Tom looked at her and said "Of course it's not disgusting why you would say such a thing". "Well she is over 40 years old surely she should not be having another baby at that age". Tom laughed and told her not to be silly and went on to say that lots of women had babies in their forties; it is nothing to be ashamed about. Ivy thought about what had had said and dried her eyes realising she was being a bit silly.

That night she got home and went into to see her mum and apologised for her outburst. "It was just a bit of a shock that's all; I never thought you would have any more babies after Rose".

On the 10 June 1933 Ivy's mother gave birth to a baby boy whom she named Leonard David. Ivy fell in love with him straight away and from that day on she cared for him as if he was her own.

A month after Len's birth on 29 July 1933 Hetty and Arthur were married Hetty had very kindly invited Ivy to be one of her maids of honour. It was such a lovely day the sun shone and everyone was happy. Hetty wore an ankle length silk wedding dress; it had a 'V' shaped neckline with ¾ length puffed sleeves. Her long veil was arranged to cover the front of her hair and was secured by a tiara-shaped headdress which sat towards the back of her head. She carried a large circular bouquet of deep red roses and white lilies finished off with long ferns trailing down the front of her dress. She had two maids of honour, her sister Jinny, and her friend Doris both of whom wore ankle length silk dresses in pale pink, and carried circular bouquets of pink roses to match their dress and Doris's 3-year old daughter Emmy who was dressed in a floor length pink frilly dress and carried a basket of mixed summer flowers.

Ivy wore a dress in slightly different design to the other two Maids of Honour it had three frills on either side of the hip of the dress and she wore a cortege of pink roses on her left shoulder. However they all wore similar head-dresses consisting of a round organza-type hat.

Arthur and Hetty went away for their honeymoon to Yarmouth for a few days. Tom was a bit upset as Hetty was his favourite sister and they were very close, but Ivy said it was nice because Tom now had an extra brother; Hetty's husband Arthur. When the newly-weds returned they settled in with nan and granddad Penn.

The following year Tom proposed to Ivy and they became engaged on her 18th birthday. Tom gave Ivy a beautiful Solitaire engagement ring and they began saving in earnest for their wedding and a home together.

Over the next 2 years they both saved hard. Ivy would buy things for her bottom drawer such as bed linen, table cloths tea towels and other items she would need for her home. Ivy's dad (granddad Betts) kept quietly in the background but he and Tom got on really well and had the same political views which they would air together. Ivy's dad had been unemployed for some time, but still managed to make a living from mending other people's shoes and of course the Betts' family shoes. Before long it become known amongst their neighbours that he could repair shoes so they began bringing their own shoes to him and asking him to carry out repairs. He would make a small charge for doing the repair and so he was soon able to eke out a meagre living, but of course every little bit of money that came into the household helped.

Ivy's mother also worked doing cleaning, washing and ironing for other people, especially the Jewish community. Although they had a large family to feed, there was always food on the table; she was a marvellous manager who could produce a meal out of practically nothing. This she passed on to her daughter Ivy telling her to never throw food away.

On one particular occasion Ivy's brother Bill had invited his mate to tea one Sunday. It was well known that their mother made lovely fruit cakes. They all sat down and enjoyed the food in front of them but for some reason that particular Sunday their mother had not done any baking. Then looking round the young lad remarked "What no 'effing' cake?" From that time on any fruit cake that their mum made was referred to as 'effing cake' and it became a family joke.

The young couple had set a date for their wedding for the 22 August 1936. They began looking for somewhere to live and finally found two rooms in Parmiter Street, Bethnal Green at a rent of 10/6d (52½p). That was quite expensive in those days, but when Tom had proposed to Ivy he had decided that he had had enough of shop fitting and had applied to the Gas Company for a job as a pipe fitter. He had to attend night classes in order to become qualified but he had done it and now he worked for the Gas Company as a pipe fitter and was paid good money so they were able to afford the rent on the two rooms. They moved all their belongings into the rooms in July and they bought some furniture on hire purchase.

A few weeks before the wedding the young couple went to a large well-known Jeweller called Spiegel's in Bethnal Green High Street to buy the wedding ring. Strangely enough, they were accompanied by her mother who had gone along to make sure that got a good deal from the Jeweller in question. Ivy chose a plain gold 22 carat band and her mother insisted that the Jeweller weigh it up to ensure that it was the correct pennyweight and that they were getting their money's worth. I couldn't imagine any bride doing that nowadays.

In the meantime, Ivy put her dressmaking skills to work and made all four bridesmaids dresses and her wedding dress. Hetty very kindly offered to loan Ivy her veil and head-dress that she had worn at her own wedding three years previously and mum accepted.

Ivy and Tom were married in St. James the Great Church known locally as The Red Church because of its distinctive red bricks. The wedding dress was ankle length and made from White satin with a high neckline and long sleeves; there was a sash around her waist which hung down at the front of the dress. To finish off the ensemble, she wore long white gloves.

She had chosen to wear Hetty's headdress and had turned it around so that the headdress sat on the front of her head and the full length veil fixed beneath it, hung down loosely over her shoulders and fell gracefully down to the floor. On her feet were white satin low heel shoes and she carried a large sheath of deep red carnations and trailing fern. The bridesmaids were dressed in pink and, lavender full length dresses with puffed sleeves.

After the wedding, the reception was held in the Church Hall; her mother had done the catering and had managed to get hold of a lovely piece of Gammon which she had boiled and sliced up. Tom's parents had also contributed some money towards the food. After the wedding the couple went back to their little home and the next day after the wedding they managed to go away for a few days. They couldn't afford a proper honeymoon but Tom promised Ivy that they would have a nice holiday later.

So they settled down to married life and were very happy. Ivy continued in her job as a machinist and Tom was doing exceedingly well in his job as a pipe fitter at the Gas Company. Later on his brother Bill was encouraged by their father to also join the Gas Company although he worked in the stores because he did not have the same qualifications as Tom.

As promised the following year Tom did take Ivy on holiday to a place called Mumbles which is a seaside resort not far from Swansea. They had some friends who lived in that area and Tom had written to them to say he and Ivy were visiting and so they very kindly offered them a room in their house.

It was the first holiday that Ivy had ever had and she did enjoy the experience. One day they were all on the beach enjoying the sunshine and Ivy decided that she would like to go in the sea. She went into one of the changing huts and put on a grey woollen swimsuit and wore a grey rubber swimming hat on her head to keep her hair dry.

Then she gingerly dipped her toes in the water which at first was very cold but as she went further into the sea, it didn't feel so bad. Soon she was enjoying swimming. Then it was time to come out and Tom came down to the water's edge with a towel to wrap around her, and jokingly said "I don't know Ivy when you go in the sea, the tide comes in". She was quite upset by this as she had put on a little bit of weight in the year that they had been married and was quite sensitive about the subject. She stalked off up the beach and Tom was left wondering what he had said, he had only meant it as a joke but Ivy hadn't seen it that way

After Ivy had changed back into her clothes he asked her what was wrong and she said "That was a nasty thing to say, I know I have put on weight but I was enjoying myself and I don't think I will ever go back into the sea again after that remark". Tom said he was sorry and hadn't meant anything by it, but true to her word, she never did go in swimming again.

They visited their friends each year and enjoyed the holidays they spent with them but true to her word Ivy never ventured in the sea, although Tom did try to persuade her.

Granddad Penn in his later years

Auntie Hettie and Uncle Arthur engagement photo.

Left: mum, bridesmaid Doris, Dad Uncle Arthur Granddad, Auntie Jinny, Nanny Penn.
Front small bridesmaid Emmy.

Uncle Arthur and Auntie Hettie's wedding 29th July 1933.

Auntie Jinny as a young woman.

Mum and Dad's wedding day 22   August 1936

CHAPTER TWO

1936 to 1944   - Early memories

Mum and Dad lived quite happily in the two rooms until on 03 September 1939 war was declared, and within a few months the German Luftwaffe were flying over London and dropping their deadly bombs leaving smouldering buildings in their wake killing many people Night after night there was a constant bombardment of bombs raining down on the city, the clang of Fire engines as they raced to put out the many fires that erupted as a result of the bombing.

Sirens would sound when enemy planes were spotted in the night sky and people would scurry to their Anderson Shelters which had been built in their back gardens, or if they were out and about the nearest Underground station offered protection. Whole families would spend the night huddled on the platforms. They would take blankets and food and spend the night not knowing what the morning would bring and in the morning many people would find that their homes had gone and they were out on the street with no-where to go. A special kind of camaraderie sprung up amongst the Londoners and entertainers would walk up and down the platform with their accordions or guitars singing the old songs encouraging folks to join in. The East End of London has always been famous for its stoic people and their ability to 'just get on with life' and take whatever it throws at them.

In October 1940, after a night of devastating raids one of the bombs that had fallen scored a direct hit on Parmiter Street with the effect that the blast blew out all the windows where mum and dad were residing. Unfortunately, mum was at home at the time and the shock of the blast left her paralysed down one side and she suffered a loss of speech She was hospitalised in the Bethnal Green Hospital where she remained for a couple of days before making a recovery.

By this time mum's family had moved from Pollard Street to number 5 Falcon Buildings in Old Bethnal Green Road.

Mum's younger siblings had been evacuated to Northampton when the bombing began but my grandmother missed them so much that she travelled to Northampton and brought them back. However she finally realised that it was just too dangerous a place for children to be in so she made the decision to move the family. So she took the younger children, Lil, Rose and Lenny and moved them to Northampton. The older children stayed in London. Bill had by now joined the army, Pete and Violet were both working in London whilst Pat, at the age of 17 joined the Women's Land Army. Meanwhile mum's father had found a job in a Munitions factory so he had to stay in London as this work was classed as vital to the war effort.

In the meantime, also realising that Bethnal Green was becoming a dangerous place in which to live dad sought other accommodation. Luckily for him my grandparents had moved from Stepney (or Mile End Old Town as it was known then) to Walthamstow just a few miles from Bethnal Green. They mentioned to dad that there were some rooms vacant a few doors away from where they lived. Dad went to see the Landlords a Mr Frank and Mrs. Ivy Stinton and arranged to rent the rooms. There were 3 in all plus an upstairs toilet.

Mum and dad salvaged what they had left of their furniture and moved into number 30 Erskine Road. The rent was 12/6d (62½p) a week which was a bit more than the rent at Parmiter Street but they did have more rooms.

Mum soon busied herself making a home for them both; she sewed new curtains and hung them at the windows, but one day as she tried to hang some curtains in the front room she overstretched and fell off the step ladder. Fortunately she only suffered bruises and she picked herself up and finished hanging the curtains making sure she moved the step ladder nearer to the window. Dad and mum were able to buy some new furniture and they soon had the flat looking like a home again.

Some two months later mum began to feel unwell and she assumed this was because she was still suffering from the shock of the bombing; so she visited my grandparents' Doctor who had a practice in Palmerston Road a short distance from their flat. Mum and dad had registered with the doctor just after they had moved to Erskine Road. His name was Doctor Goide, a pleasant man in his mid-50s so mum felt quite comfortable with him. She explained her symptoms and told him about the bombing incident and she also mentioned that she had suffered a fall but that she hadn't been seriously hurt. Dr.Goide examined her and took blood tests and urine samples and told her to return in a 2 weeks' time. In the meantime he gave her a tonic to help her.

A couple of weeks later she returned to see the doctor to get the results the tests and he surprised her with the news that she was pregnant. Dr.Goide estimated that the baby would be due around the end of October. She was so excited and could not wait to tell my dad. They had been married just over 4 years and mum had desperately wanted to start a family but had been told by another doctor who she had consulted that she would probably be unable to conceive a child because of internal problems.

Dad came home that evening and sat down and had his meal and then moved to the armchair where he opened his Daily Mirror and began to read. Mum said

"Tom, I went to the doctors today to get the results of those tests I had a couple of weeks ago and I have some exciting news, we are going to have a baby; the doctor said that it would be due around the end of October" Dad looked up from his paper and said Oh that's nice" then carried on reading. Mum was so upset at dad's cavalier attitude. I suppose it had come as a bit of a shock to him too especially as he had probably become used to the idea that they would never be parents. However he soon came around to the idea and together they went along to No.20 Erskine Road where Nan and Granddad Penn lived and imparted the news to them and to dad's 2 sisters and 3 brothers. Of course there was great excitement because the baby would be the first grandchild and the first niece or nephew.

I made my appearance in this world on the 12th November 1941 at 2.30 pm weighing in at 6lbs 4ozs. Mum told me later that it had been a cold and foggy day. Mum had gone into labour earlier that day and Nan had popped in to see how she was as she had gone past her due date. Seeing her in discomfort she had immediately arranged for her to be taken into hospital. According to my mum, she had had a dry birth and I appeared like a wizened old lady. The nurses smothered me in cream to lubricate my wrinkled skin. I was so tiny that the baby clothes mum had made for me were too big, so the nurses found some dolls clothes and put them on me. I was immediately rushed to an incubator where I spent the first hours of my life.

Dad visited the maternity ward that evening and nervously asked if he could hold me. He had not been used to tiny babies He gingerly picked me up and gazed at me in wonder, frightened that he would drop me, so mum took me off of him.

The next lot of visitors were my two uncles who were home on leave. Dad's youngest brother Ted – who was a Chef in the RAF and my mum's younger brother Bill, a despatch rider for the Army. Uncle Bill had given Uncle Ted a lift on his army motor bike, and it must have been a bit scary since it was quite thick fog at that time.

Mum left hospital after 10 days and proudly took me home to number 30 Erskine Road Walthamstow. The house was owned by Mr & Mrs. Stinton who resided in the flat downstairs, together with their daughter Evelyn.

Erskine Road itself was an exceptionally long road with rows of terraced houses either side; each house had a small front garden with a privet hedge at the front. There were roads leading off of Erskine Road to Palmerston Road which ran parallel to Erskine road on one side and roads to the market on the other. Walthamstow Market was at the bottom end of our road and number 30 was a short walking distance to the Market.

By the time I was born in November 1941 the war had been raging for over two years and London was suffering a tremendous hit with the bombing raids. We would go into Nan and granddads house when the warning siren sounded and would either retreat to the Anderson Shelter in the garden or sit beneath Nan's big wooden table which had a metal cage around it to protect us. At that time my dad's three younger brothers, Bill, Alf and Ted who still lived at home, had all enlisted in the RAF.

Being very patriotic like his brothers, Dad wanted to join the RAF too. But at that time the Recruitment Offices were only interested in enlisting young single men, and of course, dad was considered old at 28 plus he was a married man with a child.

However a year after I was born he received his call-up papers and to his utter disappointment it was not for the RAF as he had hoped, but he was seconded into the RASC

(Royal Army Service Corp) He was sent to Carlisle for his basic training from the 28th December 1942 to 8th March 1943 where he retrained as a welder. He was transferred to D Company No.3 Holding Battalion in the Royal Army Service Corp (R.A.S.C.).

As Dad was a pipe fitter by trade working for the North Thames Gas Company; his expertise as an Engineer was invaluable. Mum of course was devastated and I can just imagine how frightening it must have been for her to be left on her own with a small child. Of course my granddad was pleased about dad's secondment because he had been in the army during the First World War and had served with distinction rising to the rank of Sergeant in a very short time.

Dad came home on leave on the 12th April 1943 for 9 days, and again on 12th July and 1st November 1943.

Dad returned to his base on the 11th November a day before my 2nd birthday, and a couple of months later, to her horror, mum found that she was pregnant again. She admitted to me some years later that she hadn't planned on having another child because the future was so uncertain. To her shame she did try to procure an abortion, but fortunately this didn't work and on the 29th July 1944 she gave birth at home to a little boy weighing in at a healthy 7lbs 8 ozs, whom she called Barry Charles (Charles being dad's first name), Barry was the chubbiest baby I have ever seen, and I adored him from the moment he was born. A telegram was immediately sent to my dad telling him he had become a father for the second time. It was 7 months before he saw my brother, who by this time had begun to talk, and try as she could mum could never get him to say 'dad'. When my dad came home and held his son for the very first time, Barry looked at him and uttered the word 'dad' which amazed my mum after all her coaching to get him to say it.

Whilst mum had been pregnant with my brother Barry, my maternal grandmother - Nanny Betts - came to London and took me back with her to her home in Northampton to a village called Chelveston where I spent many happy weeks. Nan lived with my Granddad Betts, who by this time had been able to leave his job in the munitions factory and had joined Nan. He had managed to find a job on a farm which came with accommodation so they all lived in the old farmhouse.

Granddad was of slim build, not very tall, with grey hair and a pepper and salt moustache. He wore glasses behind which were a pair of twinkling blue eyes and he was always smiling showing a row of blackened and yellowing teeth which had been caused by holding the tacks in his mouth as he repaired the shoes and boots. As I was the first grandchild on both sides of the family naturally a great fuss was made of me. Granddad would stand me on the kitchen table and tell me to say a swear word "Maureen say s**t and I will give you a penny". I would shake my head and say that my mummy would tell me off. He kept on and on until I finally gave in, and with a huge grin he would press a penny into my little hand. Nan of course, would have a go at him and say "Don't teach that baby to swear it's not right and Ivy and Tom will be annoyed". He would just shrug his shoulders and say "It's only a joke", then turn and wink at me, then give me a big cuddle.

Nan was the complete opposite to granddad. They were like chalk and cheese although they seem to get along fine together. She was the strength that held the family together. Nan was a big buxom lady with white hair, a rather chubby face, with small dark blue eyes that would flash with anger if anyone upset her. To tell the truth I was a bit afraid of her. She definitely ruled the roost with a domineering manner but granddad just let her get on with it, I suspect for a peaceful life. She always wore a flowery pinafore over her dress with thick brown stockings and slippers with pom-poms on the front. In spite of her demeanour, she was very active woman and was not afraid of hard work. She grew all her own vegetables and was constantly dividing her time between digging the vegetable patch, cleaning, scrubbing and cooking not only for her own family, but for the two or three labourers who were German Prisoners-of-War who worked alongside granddad on the farm.

Mum's brothers Bill and Pete had joined the army; her sister Pat had joined the women's Land army. Violet, Lil and Rose still lived at home with Nan.

When Pat came home on a visit she would regale the family with stories of her adventures as a Land Girl. She told how she was billeted at a farm and her first job was to milk the cows. The Dairymaid showed her how to do this by pulling and squeezing the teats so the milk fell cleanly into the bucket beneath the cow. Pat thought to herself, "Well that looks easy enough". However I think she got her co-ordination wrong and instead of the milk flowing into the bucket it squirted all down her uniform. She said she could not get rid of the smell of milk for ages. No doubt she did get the hang of it eventually.

Mum's youngest brother Lenny (who would have been about 11 years old then) helped granddad on the farm after school where they worked extremely long hours. This was no 9 – 5 job not by a long stretch of the imagination, there were pigs and chickens to feed, cows to milk and all the other jobs that went with the running of a farm. The farm itself was owned by Mr.Carr who was a bit of slave driver, who never paid good wages, in spite of the work that granddad and Lenny carried out. But in those austere times a job was a job, anything that would bring a bit of extra cash into the home.

Lenny would play with me as a child and would recite a poem "Maureen Penn up the pole can't get down for a sausage roll". He still says that to me to this day whenever we meet at family events.

My Uncle Bill told me some years later when we were discussing mum's side of the family, that one weekend he had come home on leave and it was quite late at night around 9 p.m. He walked into the farmhouse and the oil lamps were lit, they had no electricity – and he asked Nan where granddad was. She replied "Oh, he is still working on the farm" Bill couldn't believe this and did no more but turned around and marched outside to the farm and the barn where granddad was still toiling away. "Hello dad – why are you still working this late?" He asked, granddad replied that Mr. Carr had given him a few jobs that had to be done that day, but they had taken a bit longer than he had anticipated. "Right dad, you are coming home with me right now – you are getting too old for this lark and you should be working proper hours not all hours of the night, I bet you haven't even stopped for something to eat have you?" Granddad shook his head and laid down his tools ready to go with Bill. As they turned to go out of the barn they bumped into Mr.Carr who had obviously come to check up to see how granddad was doing. "Where do you think you are going Betts?" he asked. Angrily Bill stepped in front of granddad and said "You effing old slave driver, he is coming 'ome with me to 'ave his dinner – he has been working all effing hours for you and what for, so that you can pay him a pittance so get out of my way before I make you". I think Mr. Carr got the message, and as they passed him he remarked "If he doesn't want to do the work I can soon find someone younger and stronger to do it for him, I only took him on out of pity". Well that was the straw that broke the camel's back because Bill turned round with his fists clenched and was about to land one on the arrogant Mr. Carr's chin when granddad stopped him. "Good luck with that, but If I 'ear you've sacked my dad, then you will answer to me" and as added as an afterthought "As for finding someone younger, you'll 'ave a bit of a job cos all the young lads 'ereabouts have been called up and if it wasn't for my dad and my younger brother Lenny, none of the work would get done, so think on". Mr Carr never did sack my granddad and I am sure his attitude changed towards him after Bill had threatened him.

One Sunday whilst staying with my grandparents my Aunt Rose offered to take me to Church with her. I must have been about 3 years old at the time and had never ever set foot in a church before; it was all so new to me. I sat quietly beside my Auntie Rose who at the age of around 14 or 15 was almost 12 years my senior. The vicar announced a few hymns which the congregation sang. Of course I didn't know any of these hymns at all and began to get a bit restless, then to Auntie Rose's horror I said in a very loud voice "When are they going to sing Mezy dotes and dozy dotes". A popular song of that time although the correct title was "Mares eat oats and does eat oats but little lambs eat ivy". To my young ears the words became muddled and I honestly thought it continued "and little tamsy-tivy". When we arrived home at the farmhouse, where my mum was staying at the time with my new brother, Rose was flushed and angry and said to mum "I'm never going to take her to church again, she showed me up". I couldn't understand what all the fuss was about; I had only asked them to sing a song that I knew.

I loved it in the farmhouse. The main road ran through the centre of the village and the farmhouse was just around the bend and lay back off the road. It had a picket fence around a very large front garden, which had flower borders around the edge, no doubt planted by my Nan and in the centre was a lawn. There was an apple tree in the corner of the garden, and when the apples were ripe Nan would pick them and make the most delicious apple pies accompanied by thick yellow custard – fair makes my mouth water to think of it.

Entering the front door of the large thatched roof farmhouse, to the right was a wide wooden staircase lovingly polished by Nan. There were three or four wide wooden steps that led to a small landing with oak panels to the right of the wooden bannister. In one of the panels was a door leading to a deep cupboard. There were many times when I would hide in there in later years when playing with my cousin Keith and Brother Barry. The stairs continued and wound round again to the second floor where there were about four bedrooms and then another staircase led to the loft where there was more sleeping accommodation. I think originally this was meant for the farm labourers of the time. I am not certain of the age of the farmhouse but even in the 1940s I guess it was pretty old.

Coming downstairs again there was a small hallway leading to a fairly large farm kitchen. It had a stone floor, and to the right was a large range on which Nan would cook the meals. On the left was a larger Welsh Dresser holding all Nan's precious china and knick-knacks. There were cupboards all around the kitchen in which she stored her provisions and cooking utensils. In the centre was an enormous wooden table which Nan would faithfully scrub clean every day, and at which everybody would gather for their meals. A door at the other end of the kitchen led out into the farmyard itself and woe betide anybody who didn't wipe their feet before entering the kitchen would receive the sharp edge of my Nan's tongue.

Nan was an excellent cook and my favourite meal was her stews with dumplings. She would bake her own bread and to accompany the stew she would cut thick slices of the bread and spread them with the butter that was made on the farm

The village was quaint with small thatched cottages in a row along the street all of which had whitened door steps. Opposite the row of cottages were the Village pub and shop. When entering the shop, my nose was immediately assailed with the different aromas of the produce sold there. There was soap for washing – usually Wrights Coal Tar Soap; Sunlight soap for scrubbing floors and was also used for washing clothes, candles, pegs metal buckets mops and brooms. At the far end of the shop was the sweet counter – my favourite part of the shop - on the shelf above the counter were rows and rows of sweets in big glass jars. The elderly lady who ran the shop was a kindly soul and when I visited the shop with my grandmother she would take down one of the big jars of sweets and weigh them up on a set of old-fashioned brass scales and tip the sweets onto a square piece of paper then twist it. "There you are my dear" she would say. She would never take any money for the sweets.

I also got quite friendly with another resident of the village who lived in one of the cottages next door to the farmhouse. She was quite an elderly lady, who lived on her own and was a regular church goer. I am afraid to say that I was quite naughty, as I used to sit on her lovely whitened step and when I needed to go to the toilet I would just wee myself and of course it would go all over the step. My Nan would be very cross with me, but the old lady, would say "Don't scold her she is only a baby". I must have been about two and half then.

When mum had had my brother she brought him to the village so that she could recuperate and I had time to bond with him. Barry's Identity Card was actually registered in Chelveston shortly after his birth. Then after a few weeks, mum decided to go back to London, but my Nan insisted on going back with her until she had fully recovered from Barry's birth. Upon arriving at our flat Nan looked around and commented that it needed doing up. She was a dab hand at painting and very resourceful being able to turn her hand to anything. Without further ado, she took herself to the local Market and came back with a large pot of green paint. She proceeded to cover up everything in the room with old sheets to protect the furniture and told my mum to go along to her in-laws (my other grandparents) whilst she set about painting the walls with this green paint and the skirting boards and woodwork in white.

When we returned several hours later it was all done. Nan stayed with us for a couple of weeks, and then said that she must go back as granddad needed her.

Bethnal Green

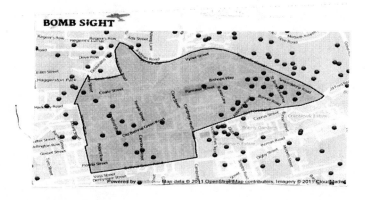

Map showing where the bomb hit on Parmiter Street

Dad's army pay book

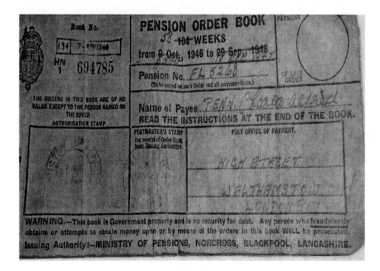

Dad's pension Order book

Dad in army uniform

Mum with Barry aged 7 months and Maureen Aged 3 years.

*Maureen aged 3 years old and below
Maureen with her baby brother Barry aged 7 months.*

Above Uncle Ted and Uncle Alf in RAF uniform
Below: Uncle Bill in the RAF

CHAPTER THREE

1944 – 1945 – Barry and Me

Barry grew very fast and he was soon toddling around on his little fat legs. Nan and Granddad Penn made a lot of fuss of him; he was such a loving little boy. He was always giving my mum cuddles and he would to say to her that when he grew up he would marry her.

In May 1945 the war came to an end but our dad was not demobbed from the army until the end of the year on the 5th December. There were many street celebrations everywhere with all the neighbours getting together and assembling long tables down the street, using their ration coupons and somehow managing to put on a big feast. Of course my brother Barry doesn't remember because he was only about 10 months old and still a 'babe in arms'

Rationing had been instigated in 1940 to prevent the Germans starving the British people out. People were encouraged to grow their own produce. Items such as butter, sugar, bacon, meat and cheese were rationed, and ration books were issued for each member of the family containing coupons and these could be exchanged at designated shops.

In June 1941 clothes were also put on ration as was tea, jam biscuits, cereals eggs, lard canned and dried fruit and potatoes. Petrol was also rationed. In mid-1946 bread was rationed then taken off rationing in 1948. In 1949 clothes were taken off rationing and in 1950 petrol rationing ended. February 1953 saw sweets taken off rationing, and finally in September 1953 it was sugar. By 4th July 1954 everything came off rationing. In spite of the hard times, Barry and I had a lovely childhood. We were always in and out of our Nan and Granddad Penn's house. It was pretty crowded as both of uncles Alf and

Ted had returned from the war together with my Uncle Bill. My Auntie Het and her husband Arthur, who had got married in 1933, had finally moved out to a flat of their own in Springfield Road in another part of Walthamstow. The house at number 20 Erskine Road was quite large with a lovely garden which my uncle Ted lovingly tended as he was a keen gardener. He was one of my favourite Uncles and he always had time for me and would teach me about growing flowers and general gardening and I was allowed to help him whenever I was there. He was a Chef by trade and after the war he had returned to his job in a posh hotel in London. At that time he was going out with a young lady called Winnie and they were engaged to be married. Winnie asked me if I would like to be a bridesmaid and of course, I was overjoyed at the idea. She asked me if I would like to wear a lavender dress, as this was her favourite colour. I had no idea what *'Lavender'* looked like, but said yes anyway.

Uncle Ted and Winnie would take me everywhere, we went to the zoo, and places of interest in London, although I can't say I remembered much of that but I do remember on one occasion when they took me to the Cinema to see Uncle Tom's Cabin, and whenever I heard the song *'Zibberty doo-da Zibberty-day, my oh my what a wonderful day, plenty of sunshine coming my way, Zibberty-do-da, Zibberty day'* I remember that film and how much I enjoyed the story and the music.

Suddenly Winnie wasn't around anymore and nobody told me why but Uncle Ted seemed to go around looking very sad all the time. He lost interest in his garden and used to go out on long walks by himself. He didn't even want to play our favourite game with me which was to stick two pieces of paper on his forefinger and middle finger then pronounce *'two little dicky birds sitting on the wall, one named Peter and one named Paul'* then he would lift both fingers up and away and continue 'Fly away Peter, fly away Paul' and put two fingers down without the bits of paper on them then they would magically appear again when he sang 'Come back Peter come back Paul'. It took me a long time to figure out how he did that but I would always ask him to do it again.

Uncle Ted was a good-looking man and I guess he was in his late twenties by this time. Winnie was tall and slim with long brown curly hair. She had bulging eyes which mum said was caused through a Goitre - I had no idea what that was. I took her word for it, I grew quite fond of Winnie and I think she was fond of me also.

Of course I found out many years later that all the time Uncle Ted had been away he had been sending money home to Winnie to put away for their wedding. He had also brought back from abroad a length of white silk to be made into a wedding dress for her. Apparently she had taken all the money and run off with someone else. I never did know what happened to her. All I know is that it broke Uncle Ted's heart and he never recovered and stayed single for the rest of his life until he died at the age of 65 from a heart attack and lung cancer.

At that time the streets were kept spotless by various men coming round with barrows sweeping all the debris and dead leaves up and placing them in the barrow to take back to the depot. Unlike nowadays when the streets are filthy with peoples discarded food boxes and all kinds of rubbish.

There was one particular man called Harry who would go round cleaning our street and sweeping up any debris. Barry and I got to know him and would chat away to him whenever he got to our house. Mum also got to know him quite well and would pass the time of day with him. Harry had quite a soft spot for Barry and would allow Barry to help him; he even gave Barry a little broom of his own. Barry would accompany Harry to the top of the road sweeping all the rubbish and putting it in the Harry's barrow. He absolutely loved it, and I can still see him now dressed in his little blue dungarees and sandals.

One day after he had been helping Harry, unknown to our Mum, he had gone along to our grandparent's house and knocked on the door, when Nan opened the door he was standing on the doorstep with a dead pigeon in his hands. "Here you are Nan; I brought you a chicken for your dinner". Nan was of course horrified, but didn't let Barry know; she just took the dead bird off of him and took him into the house and washed his hands. I don't know what happened to the bird, no doubt it was dumped in the dustbin, but my Nan later related the story to my mum and they had a good laugh about it.

To distinguish between the two sets of grandparents, we called my dad's parents Little Nanny and Big Granddad and my mother's parents big Nanny and Little Granddad for obvious reasons of their sizes in relation to each other.

As mentioned previously, Nan and Granddad Penn lived just five doors away from us at number 20 Erskine Road. It was a large house with a fairly large front garden which was tiled leading up to the two steps to the front door. There was a thick privet hedge all around the front of the house. The hall was quite dark with brown embossed Anaglyptic wallpaper on the walls going right up the stairs. On the right hand side of the hall, there was a door which led into the *parlour*. This room was always kept for best for visitors so the furniture was highly polished and everything was dusted and kept clean. We would also spend many Christmas nights in there when Uncle Alf would dress up as Father Christmas and unknown to me and my brother, he would go outside and then knock on the door and would bringing in a big sack of toys.

A flight of stairs led up to the 4 bedrooms, one of which had a toilet leading off of the room that was my Auntie Jinny's room.

There were three other bedrooms the front one being my Nan and Granddads room. Thinking about it, I am amazed where they all slept when my dad's 3 brothers lived there together with my Aunt Het (dad's eldest sister) and her husband Arthur.

Downstairs was a large back room and leading off of this was the scullery. There was a white-washed boiler in the corner, where Nan would spend all day every Monday doing her laundry.

Nan always wore pair of old brown slippers and because she suffered with bunions, which were huge and must have been painful at times, she had to cut holes in the slippers to allow the bunions to protrude. I think that when she wore outdoor shoes she had to first have them stretched to accommodate the bunions. In spite of this, my Nan was a happy person and was always chuckling about something. She had a lot of time of my brother and me and would slip us little treats. I loved her dearly and I still miss her to this day.

Her only vices were her cigarettes and a glass of whisky, or glass of stout every now and again. For such a little woman she was extremely wiry and strong and each Monday she would sort out the whites from the colours and using her wooden tongs, she would haul the clothes and bed linen that had to be washed into the big white copper, under which a fire had been lit early in the morning to heat up the water. On wet days and winter time there would be a wooden drier slung across the ceiling suspended on hooks either side of the scullery on which she hung the damp clothes. There was a rope at the side which she used to lower the drier and once the clothes were hung upon it, she would haul it up again and tie the rope around a hook on the wall. On dry and windy days the washing would be hung out on the line in the garden.

On the right of the scullery was a large white butler sink with a wooden draining board, and hanging on the wall by the side of the sink was her scrubbing board. She used this to scrub any clothes which had any awkward stains or dirt on them before placing them in the boiler She would then stir the clothes around with her wooden 'dolly', which was like a large wooden spoon made for that purpose and when she considered that they were clean, she would then heave the wet hot washing into a large basket and take it all out to the lean-to where she had a mangle. A bucket would be placed on the other side of the mangle to catch the water as the clothes were put through. One by one she would pick up the wet clothes with big wooden tongs and feed them between the two large rollers of the mangle turning the rollers via a large handle at the side. She would do this two of three times to get most of the water out of them, and then they would be hung out in the garden if it was fine, or on the wooden drier in the scullery.

Unlike nowadays this was heavy work and took the whole day. Then of course she ironed them the next day. She had two irons and they had to be heated by standing them on the range where she had a lit a fire. She would rub the bottom of the iron with a cloth on which she had put beeswax. As soon as one iron cooled she would place it on the range to heat up and use the second iron, and that is how she continued until she had a neat pile of clothes all ironed and ready to put away.

Before my brother made his appearance mum would often go round to Nan and Granddads in the summer and sit in the garden, as she was not allowed to do so in the garden belonging to the house where we lived because

Mrs. Stinton, was so proud of her plants that would not allow me out into the garden for fear I would trample on them and damage or break them. She did allow mum out there one day a week just to hang out the washing. One particular Sunday Mum was helping Nan shell some peas and I was playing as usual. I had been given a toffee to keep me quiet when all of a sudden I swallowed it but it became stuck in my throat. The next thing I knew I was being turned upside down and held by my feet and was being thumped hard on my back until the toffee dropped out. Luckily my Uncle Arthur had been sitting in the kitchen washing his feet when he had heard me choking and acted swiftly and I believe he saved my life that day. This tale was related to me by my mum who said she just burst into tears. I must have been about 2 at the time.

Nan and Granddad had a dog called Peggy. She was a little Heinz 57 mongrel and was so placid. Mum said when I was a baby I would play with Peggy, she would sit there whilst I dressed her up in dolls clothes. However one day I think she had had enough and I went just that little bit too far; I had been hanging on her tail, which must have been very painful. She did no more but turned round and delivered a nasty bite on my mouth. I think I learned my lesson after that and never teased her again.

After the war when everyone returned to their Civvie jobs, Uncle Alf started a hobby of making boats. He spent hours in Nan and Granddad cellar flattening out old cocoa tins and he produced a beautiful model of the Queen Mary. He made all the little life boats that were on the side of the boat and it was an excellent replica. He sold it to a model shop in Walthamstow Market and we would often go past and see it displayed in the window. I don't know whether anyone bought it but it was on show for an awful long time.

He also made a larger boat, but realised too late that it was too big to get out of the cellar so he had to dismantle it before bringing it up and placing it in the garden where he assembled it once again. This boat was more like a kind of canoe. I remember that quite often the cellar would flood and Uncle Alf would have to bail it out and then let it dry naturally. If I was naughty my Nan would threaten to lock me in the cellar. The thought of that scared the life out of me, so I always made sure that I behaved myself when I was visiting my grandparents.

I was a happy little girl and enjoyed playing with my brother although sometimes we did argue. One day I overheard mum talking to Mrs. Stinton downstairs. It was a general conversation about the weather and so on then my ears pricked up. Mrs. Stinton was saying that her daughter Evelyn was growing up so fast and she wondered if mum would like Evelyn's doll's pram for me. So mum said that was very kind and she was sure I would love it. I was very excited and couldn't wait for the day when I could have the pram. It stood in the downstairs hallway outside Mr & Mrs Stinton's flat. It was dark blue with a hood and a pram cover and I thought it would be lovely and I had just the dolly that would look good in the pram.

Days went by then weeks and I still didn't have this precious doll's pram, until one day I decided to take matters into my own hands. So carefully going downstairs I took hold of the handle of pram and pulled it towards me and the stairs and then proceeded to haul it up the steps one by way. I had probably reached the second or third stair when mum hearing all the noise came out and saw what all the noise was about. "Maureen, what do you think you are doing, put that dolls pram back at once it doesn't belong to you does it?" I did as I was told and replied "Well Mrs. Stinton said I could have it and I have been waiting for such a long time, so I didn't think she would mind if I took it". Well I never did get the pram; I guess I burnt my bridges when I had tried to take it for myself.

The boat built by Uncle Alf and below Nan And Granddad's Dog Peggy.

Winters were always cold with snow, ice and fog and summers always seemed to be so hot that the tar melted in the roads. I was quite a friendly child and would chat to anybody, much to my mum's annoyance. One particular Sunday, I must have been around 4½ years old; Barry and I were playing outside the house when a man approached us. He started chatting to us, I responded but Barry ran indoors. "Do you like animals?" he asked. I replied that I did. Then he said "Have you ever been to a zoo?" I said that I had and that my aunt and uncle had taken me. "Well, would you like to go again?" Of course I said yes. So taking my hand he led me along Somers Road which was the turning at the side of my house, and then at the top of Somers road, we turned right into Westbury Road, walked down the length of this road and then left into the Walthamstow Market.

There were a lot of bombed out buildings still evident from the war which were slowly being rebuilt. He took me up to the top of the High Street where we crossed over the main road and on the corner opposite was the bombed out building that used to be Burtons the Tailors. The man let go of my hand and urged me to follow him into the building where he promptly undid his trousers and urinated up the wall. I looked away not sure what to do. He took hold of my hand and said "Let's go to the zoo now". We walked a long way up a hill, which I now know was Church Hill and turning right at the top we came to St. Mary's Church. This is the oldest church in Walthamstow having been built in around 11th or 12th century. There are many family tombs dotted around an overgrown graveyard some of which contain the remains of well-known people. Once there he took me behind some gravestones which were thickly overgrown with bushes and weeds and putting his arms around me he lifted my dress and attempted to take down my panties. I was absolutely terrified and struggled to get free, I kicked him and he let go, and I ran down the path the way the man had taken me and was crying not sure where to go from there. Fortunately a couple of Girl Guides were walking along who I believe had been attending church and they stopped me and asked me what was the matter. Sobbingly I told them what had happened, and they asked me if I knew where I lived. I knew it was 30 Erskine Road as mum and drummed this into my head.

They took me home and knocked on the door and my poor mum who had been out of her mind with worry, since Barry had gone indoors and told her about the man, opened the door. The two girls explained what had happened, and mum could not thank them enough.

She got Barry and put him in his pram and went along to Nan and Granddad's house; by this time she was in tears and really shaken up. Nan tried to comfort her but mum was also shaking with anger. She had put dad's hammer in the bottom of the pram and together with Nan and my Uncle Ted they retraced my footsteps all along until they came to the church hoping that the man would still be hanging around. I dread to think what would have happened to him had mum got hold of him. Needless to say, he had been long gone. So that was my lesson not to talk to strangers.

As mentioned previously, we spent a lot of our holidays in the summer months with our Nan and Granddad Betts in Northants. Auntie Violet, Auntie Rose and Auntie Lil still lived at home and they were all working, mainly in local factories.

Auntie Violet was a very outgoing kind of a girl and on her weekends off, she would attend the local village dances, which also attracted a large number of American Servicemen who were stationed on an Aerodrome outside the village. One day Violet came home very upset and in tears and had to tell my Nan that she was pregnant. Of course when this happened to the English girls the American Army closed ranks and more often or not, the offending soldier was sent back home.

Auntie Violet gave birth to a boy on the 18th June 1944, (a month before my brother was due to be born) whom she named Keith. Mum was a bit annoyed by this as that was the name she had chosen should she have had a boy. So when my brother was born on 29th July she chose the name 'Barry' which I believe had been her second choice of names.

Uncle Bill told me years later that he had come home on leave and found out about Violet's pregnancy and who had put her in the *'family way'*. Without telling Nan and Granddad, Bill and his brother Pete had jumped on Bill's motor bike and rode to the American Airbase. They managed to get past the guard with some excuse as they were both in army uniform. Parking up the bike he asked one of the American soldiers where this particular man was. Bill and Pete found the man and grabbed hold of him and in Bill's words *'knocked ten barrels of s**t out of him'* before being dragged off by the Red Caps – which were Military Police. They were hauled in front of the Officer in charge and asked for an explanation. Bill angrily told him that this man had made his sister pregnant and was not going to stand by her. They were both read the riot act; they were then turned over to the British Military unit and given 10 days in the glasshouse. This was a very common occurrence during and after the war and no doubt the Officer concerned had heard it all before. Nothing more was heard of the soldier in question and he was probably repatriated back to the States.

We got to play with our cousin Keith when we visited our grandparents, and had many adventures once getting lost outside the village and our uncle Lenny had to come and find us. Once again I was in for a telling off as I was the eldest and this was to continue all through my childhood. I always had a sense of adventure and no matter how often I got into trouble, pretty soon it would be forgotten and I would move on to the next adventure.

When our holiday was over we would all travel back to London and I would wish that I was back in Chelveston again.

At the old farmhouse standing: 2 German prisoners-of war Auntie Rose centre l to r Granddad, Uncle Lenny, Nanny Betts, Auntie Violet, Uncle Bill and front cousin Keith.

Above: Uncle Ted as a chef

Nan Peggy and Uncle Alf in the garden at Erskine Road Walthamstow. Winnie and Uncle Ted.

Above: Dad with Uncle Alf in the garden at Erskine Road

Below: Auntie Jinny on the doorstep of 20 Erskine Road.

The street party for VE day around 1945

Below: Nanny Penn on holiday in Yarmouth

Barry outside No. 30 Erskine Road
Aged about 3 years old.

Above: Dad's discharge papers

Below: Identity Cards

CHAPTER FOUR

1945 – 1948 School days

The years flew past pretty quickly and at 5 years old it was time for me to go to school. Mum had enrolled me at Mission Grove School which was in a turning off of the High Street. I clearly remember my first day, I was tearful and didn't want mum to leave me. All the children were assembled in a large dimly lit hall with a high ceiling from which hung several electric lights with white or cream glass shades. The children were all separated into classes and a teacher took hold of my hand and led me away. I was told to hold the hand of the little girl next to me and we were taken into our classroom. It was a big room, fairly dark with rows of desks and to get to the back row one had to go up about 3 steps, so the desks were actually in tiers.

Our first day was spent drawing and playing and then it was lunchtime and mum was outside with my brother in the pram and we went home for lunch. When we returned we played for a while then we were told that we all had to have an afternoon nap and were taken into a room in which there were several trestle beds. I am not certain how long these 'naps' were but I do remember that when we returned to our classroom it was story time. We all sat very still whilst our teacher read a story. I think that is where I learned to love books and stories, as I got older and was able to read for myself, I always had my nose stuck in a book. My mum used to call me a bookworm. I wasn't sure what that meant and imagined a worm sitting on a chair with a pair of glasses reading a book.

The school would have drama classes and towards the end of my first year, they put on a play called Hansel and

Gretel. All the children took part in one way or another. I was chosen to be the wicked witch and the parents were asked to make costumes for the children. As mentioned previously mum was an excellent needlewoman as this had been her trade before we had come along. She made me a long black cloak fastened at the neck with ties, and a tall black pointed hat on which she had cut out silver stars and moons. She had attached piece of elastic to the brim which went beneath my chin to keep the hat on. I was so proud of my outfit.

We were all very excited when the day came to perform in front of our parents and in some cases, our grandparents.

We got to the part where I had trapped the children in my house. The 'house' was formed by a ring of children all holding hands, Hansel and Gretel were trying to escape and I was meant to try and stop them, then the boy playing Hansel gave me an almighty push, I toppled over and my lovely witches hat fell over my eyes. Everybody laughed but I just felt so embarrassed and burst into tears. I have never forgotten that terrible moment, although looking back now, it must have been funny.

In May time the school held a competition for the May Queen. I was so desperate to become the May Queen, but a much prettier girl was chosen. We were taught how to dance around the Maypole which had been erected in the school playground. That was fun and I did enjoy that.

There were darker moments during my early schooldays which terrified me. When it came to making friends, I was a bit shy. I recall that I needed to go to the toilet really badly. The toilets were situated outside at the end of the playground. However there were a few older children with whom I had not got on with very well, and one day I needed to use the toilet, one of the girls waited until I entered the toilet and with the help of others they locked me in and wouldn't let me out. Since that day, I have had a fear of enclosed spaces and being in the dark and I panic. I was crying and screaming begging them to let me out, and it was only when a teacher came along, hearing all the noise that she realised what had happened. Those children were severely told off; I would not retaliate and would just run away. I would try to hold myself rather than ask to go to the toilet and as a result I would often wet myself. Mum would be exasperated when I kept coming home with wet underwear. In the end she took me to the doctors to find out why I kept wetting myself Of course I didn't tell my mum about the other children which on reflection perhaps if I had done it would have saved me a lot of grief. The Doctor told mum to monitor what I drank and at that time I had a particular fondness for Camp Coffee. This was in a tall thin bottle and was a thick brown liquid to which you added hot water and carnation milk. The doctor said not to give that to me. It didn't help at all and I continued to have problems, and of course, children being children they can be rather cruel if one of their number is slightly different so I was ribbed something terrible.

I did have one friend who stayed with me and her name was Hilda. She was a little Jewish girl who lived in the same road as us and she too was ostracised by some of the children, so we both clung together and became firm friends.

I was invited to have tea at her house and they gave me sandwiches with a very strange spread on them which I found out was Peanut butter and it was absolutely delicious. I badgered my mum to buy some which I think she did in the end to shut me up.

As we grew older we ventured further and although my mum had warned me not to go too far, being me and a stroppy little madam, I took my brother's hand and together with our friends who lived up the road, Michael and Eileen Ebbles, we walked up the market. At the top of the market on the right hand side was the old Swimming baths, where people could to have their weekly baths which would cost tuppence and included a towel and a piece of soap.

Before the Swimming baths on the same side of the road there was an old building which I believe used to be the old George Monoux College. It had suffered some bomb damage during the war and like many buildings was left derelict. That was a place to explore. We all used to wriggle in through a broken railing and would roam the overgrown grounds and it was fun, until the day that we got caught. We knew that there was a Caretaker who used to look after the buildings and the surrounding grounds, but we had never seen him until this particular day. We had been playing quite happily then I said "I think we should be going home now, it must be nearly tea time because my tummy is rumbling". So one by one first Michael, then Eileen then Barry squeezed through the broken railing. I was about to do the same when I felt a hand grab my shoulder. It was the dreaded Caretaker. "Come here you little nuisance, I'll teach you to trespass you know you aren't supposed to be here". I struggled to get free but he held on tight. "Right, I'm going to tell the police that you have been here and do you know what they will do to you? They will lock you up in a cell with bread and water and throw away the key, so you won't see your mum and dad anymore" By this time, I was crying and pleading to him to let me go. "Please mister let me go, I promise I won't come here again, I don't want to be locked up". To my surprise he did let me go and I quickly squeezed through the railings and we all ran home. I never went back.

About this time I had a friend called Jean Clark who lived in Eldon Road which was a turning further down near the market off of Erskine Road with whom I had made friends at school. We were walking to school one day when she told me that her mum was going to join her to the Girls Brigade who met in the hall next to her house. I had never heard of the Girls Brigade before and asked her all about it. "Why don't you ask you mum if you can join too" she said. So when I got home that afternoon I did ask mum. She wanted to know a bit more about it so the next day mum and I went along to Jean's house and mum spoke to her mother and she liked what she heard and said that I could join. I think at that time she would have done almost anything to keep me from getting into mischief. So the next week mum took me to Jean's house at 6 o'clock and Jean and I together with our mums went next door to the Girls Brigade meeting.

My first impression was a large hall with a table at the far end at which sat three women. The new recruits were all lining up with their parents who were filling in some forms. It was soon our turn. Jean's mum went first and she was asked to fill in name and address date of birth and so on. Then mum and I had to do the same.

When all the recruits had been enrolled the parents were asked to sit down and one of the women, who appeared to be the leader, stood up and explained what the Girls Brigade were all about. She said that the girls were taught all kinds of skills such as needlework, woodcraft and art and craft. They also arranged outings to various places of interest for a small fee. Girls who had joined that night would be asked to come every week for 4 weeks to see if they liked it and if they fitted in they would be officially enrolled and the parents could buy them a uniform. This consisted of a dark blue dress buttoned up to the collar with a brown belt and a yellow scarf tied around the neck. They would meet every Tuesday at 6 o'clock until 8 o'clock and then parents would come along and collect their children.

She also explained that we would be expected to attend Church on a Sunday morning and all Girls would assemble outside the hall at 9 a.m. sharp and then would march to the Church at the Top of the market called Marsh Street Congregational Church. The service started at around 10 a.m. and lasted an hour. (I didn't much fancy this part of it very much, as I remembered my experience in a church when I went with my Auntie Rose). Still I would give it a go.

So Jean and I faithfully attended the hall each Tuesday and I must say I did enjoy most of the activities. Of course to be able to go on the outings we had to be fully fledged members. I also enjoyed the march up to the church because people would stop and look at us as we went by and I felt quite important. What I didn't like was sitting in the drafty old church and the service seemed to go on and on. Also I still had my bladder problem so I would be bursting to go to the toilet by the end of the service.

After about 5 weeks or so, Jean said she didn't want to go anymore I didn't really want to go on my own so I too gave it up. Mum was a bit disappointed that I didn't want to attend anymore but she was ok about it afterwards.

The market itself was established in 1885 and at that time was known as 'Marsh Street'. It was and still is the longest market in Europe being a kilometre long or just under a mile. It was a real market in those days with all kinds of stalls which included fruit and vegetable, haberdashery stalls, sweet stalls, stalls selling handbags, gloves and hats. There were a few big stores too. There was a Marks and Spencer's at the bottom half of the High Street (that is now Lidl's), and a Green Stores or what became British Home Stores (BHS) over on the other side of the road, which is now an Argos store. We also had a small Sainsbury's shop not a supermarket but an old fashioned shop with assistants serving the customers. Next to that was an offal shop where mum would buy Cow Heel and Tripe. To think I used to eat that when I was a kid, I couldn't do it now, I suppose tastes change and we had to have what we got. Food was still on ration and the last thing to come off of ration was sweets in the early 1950s.

Our favourite shop was Manzes where they sold pie and mash and eels and mash with liquor. They had a stall outside the shop where there were about three large steel containers in which live eels wriggled around and we kids would watch to see if any of them tried to escape. If one of the eels slithered over the top of the container, the man would just pick it and throw it back in with the other eels. People would choose the eels they wanted and the man would pick them up with his leather gloves and place them on the chopping board and chop them up whilst they were alive, and the sections would still be wriggling. Us kids would be fascinated by them and stand for ages watching. Later on of course, it was banned for being cruel. When I was around 7 years old, mum would give me some money and Barry and I would go to[1] Manzes and have pie and mash or if mum didn't have a lot of money just mash and liquor. It was delicious and Manzes was well known for their Pie and Mash. Mr.Manze himself came to England from Italy and set up the shop in around 1925 and it is still there to this day. It was a narrow shop with a black and white tiled floor. There were white and green tiles on the walls, and it always appeared to be dark in there even though there were several lights hanging from the ceiling. On the left was the long high counter,

---

[1] Manzes was awarded Heritage status in November 2013

which at that age I could barely see over and had to stand on tiptoe to hand over the money. On the right were the booths with tables and benches where you would sit to eat your meal. A lady was always going round collecting the empty plates and wiping the tables before the next customer sat down. On each table was a bottle of vinegar with chillies in the bottom and salt and pepper.

You ordered your pie and mash and paid for it then moved along the counter to where there were trays containing knives, forks and spoons. They didn't sell drinks at that time, but they did sell gorgeous fruit pies which I think were about 3d (1½p). Sometimes mum would give us the money so we could get a fruit pie each, but not very often.

I would collect our knives and forks and find a booth in which to sit down and would leave Barry there to save our seats whilst I went back and got our dinner. This was our treat on a Friday dinner time. Later on of course, we went up in the world and had Fish and Chips but that is another story.

Every Saturday we would go to Saturday morning pictures at the Granada in Hoe Street. We would meet up with our friends and off we would go. There would be a long queue which stretched around the alleyway close to the cinema. Then we would be enthralled at the cowboy and Indian films all shouting for the goodies and booing the baddies. There would be some cartoons and in the interval a man would be sitting on a giant organ which rose from the floor and another man would come on to the stage and we would all have a sing song. He would then ask the audience if there were any children who had birthdays, and of course everyone would scramble onto the stage where they would receive goody bags. It was a good couple of hour's entertainment and it got us out of our mum's hair for a while.

Then we would come out of the cinema and turn down the alleyway to go home. At the bottom of the alley were stables that housed the horses who pulled the milk floats and bread vans. We would watch whilst the blacksmith shoed the horses, or we would go and stroke the horses as they put their heads over the stable doors. In those days, horse and carts were used extensively for pulling the Milk floats or the Bakers Vans. The horses were so familiar with the rounds that the baker or the milkman would jump down off of the cart deliver the milk or bread and the horse would continue on to the next house.

There were big Shire horses that would pull the coal carts. They would go along the street delivering coal to the houses. The driver would wear a black hood over his head and shoulders, and several layers of coats, they always wore their belts with the buckles at the back this was to prevent the buckles digging into their stomachs as they lifted the heavy coal sacks and also to also prevent the coal sacks getting caught up on the buckle. You could hardly see the coalman's face as it would be covered in black coal dust. He would lift the big bags of coal onto his shoulders and carry them into the house and tip them into the coal cupboards or coal 'oles as they were known. I would hate to have been the lady who washed the clothes.

There was of course other entertainment for us children. They had a theatre in the top half of the Market called The Palace. They would put on adult shows which my dad and his brothers would go to watch. We would look at the photos outside, and I recall that there was one show with a lady called 'Jane' appearing in it with her sausage dog called Fritz. She was always in a state of undress with lacy underwear, and a cartoon was created from her character and appeared in the Daily Mirror, which I used to grab hold of when my dad had finished reading it because I liked the cartoons in there.

Around December and January time The Palace would put on Pantomimes and charged 6d (2½p) for children. Barry and I together with Michael and Eileen would pay our money and climb up the stairs to the Gods where we would enjoy Pantomimes like Cinderella, Sleeping Beauty and Puss in Boots, shouting as loud as the other kids at the villains.

During the winter of 1946/1947 I suffered greatly with colds and abscesses in my ears giving me terrible earaches and sore throats and although my mum would take me to the doctors each time for medicine to relieve the symptoms they came back. Finally Doctor Goide decided enough was enough and when examining my throat after another bout of earaches and a sore throat he said I had yet another abscess in my ear and that my tonsils were almost closed up and would have to come out. He told my mum that once that was accomplished then the problems with my ears should clear up.

So Doctor Goide arranged for me to be admitted to Connaught Hospital in Orford Road, Walthamstow. My parents came with me bringing Barry with them and settled me down in a long ward of beds which contained other sick children. I was very nervous and tearful having never been away from my mum and dad before especially in hospital. My operation was the next day and the Doctor had seen me previously and explained that I would have a rather nasty sore throat after the operation but it would soon clear up.

Soon I was back in the ward and awoke to find a nurse by my bedside. I was feeling very woozy and the nurse told me not to try to speak. She left me to regain consciousness fully then came back with a large bowl of jelly. She said it would soothe my sore throat. Well I was in heaven as during the following few days I had jelly, ice-cream and soup all of which went down my throat really easily. I was in hospital around 6 days by which time I had begun to eat more solid foods and soon my mum and dad came to collect me to take me home. Barry held on to my hand and said that he had missed me and promised that he wouldn't annoy me anymore. That lasted all of one day.

Doctor Goide had been correct in his diagnosis because after the removal of my Tonsils I never suffered from abscesses in my ears or a sore throat again.

In November 1947 my dad's brother Bill who was the fourth eldest of Nan and Granddad's children married Lillian Markwell at St.Edwards Parish Church in Leyton London E10. It was a very cold day and both Barry and I were wrapped up warmly. I had a brick coloured coat and hat on with thick stockings to keep me warm with a thick scarf around my neck. Barry was dressed likewise but he had a pair of warm trousers on. After the wedding they had a small reception on the church hall. Bill and Lil didn't go away on honeymoon as money was still a bit tight, but they moved in with Nan and Granddad and took over the back parlour and had one of the bedrooms upstairs.

My Uncle Bill worked for the same Gas Company as my dad, but he was in the Stores whilst my dad was a 'Pipe Fitter' (or a Plumber as it is known today). My Aunt Lil was nice enough although she was a bit domineering whilst Uncle Bill was very placid They had met when Uncle Bill was in the RAF and aunt Lil was in the WAAF's I believe she worked in the administration as a typist

Within a few months of their wedding Aunt Lil was pregnant and so we were to have a little cousin to play with soon.

Marsh Street Church which I attended with the Girl Guides.

Walthamstow High Street circa 1937 showing the old Monoux building on the left and the Palace Theatre on the right

CHAPTER FIVE

1948 – 1949 – Friends and Adventures

As we got older Barry and I were allowed to play out in the street just as long as we didn't stray too far. Our friends Michael and Eileen Ebbles lived just up the road from us and we would go up to their house and sit on the doorstep. Their grandmother lived with them and she used to make the most gorgeous home-made chips and wrap them in newspaper and bring them out to us.

At the bottom of our road was a removal firm called 'Dawsons'. The owner was an elderly man (at least he looked elderly to our young eyes) who always wore a black jacket, a white shirt, a black waistcoat and striped trousers. Across the waistcoat was a fob watch, which he was constantly checking because he was a stickler for time-keeping and I suspect a strict employer.

A high whitewashed wall surrounded the offices of Dawson's which was ideal to play ball games against that is until a very angry Mr.Dawson appeared and told us to clear off. We did as we were told, but as soon as Mr.Dawson went back into his office we were back bouncing our balls off of his lovely white wall. He must have got sick and tired of telling us.

Barry and I would visit Nan and Granddad Penn, and granddad would always be sat in his wooden rocking chair in the back room. I was wary of him because he was such a big man with this large bushy moustache and a booming voice which of course had served him well in the Army during the First World War as a Sergeant, no doubt the men soon stood to attention when he opened his mouth to speak. He stood about 5ft 10" or so, not very tall by today's standards, but he was also big and muscular, he quite swamped my little Nan when she stood by his side.

Barry however adored granddad and was not a bit afraid of him.

We would both sit on little stools at Granddad's feet and Barry would chat away to him. For some reason Granddad had given Barry a nickname of *'Dicky Di-do'*. Goodness knows where that came from, but he would eventually put his hand in his pocket and give us a three-penny bit each and say "Go on go down to Tony's and get an ice-cream". I must explain that Tony's was an ice-cream parlour in our local high street which was about 5 minutes' walk from our grandparents' house and they did the most delicious ice-cream I have ever tasted. We would happily trot off to Tony's and buy our ice-cream cones.

Sometimes Barry wouldn't wait for granddad to give him the three penny-piece he would say "Granddad mummy won't give me any money for ice-cream" and of course granddad would put his hand in his pocket and hand us one each. That is until mum found out about it and Barry got an awful telling off, she told my granddad that he was not to give Barry money if he had asked for it, to which our granddad replied that he was only a nipper and he didn't mind him asking for money after all surely she didn't begrudge him giving his grandchildren pocket money. So we still used to get our three-penny piece each.

Once the war was over and dad had returned to his job at the North Thames Gas Company, he would normally take his summer holidays in the first two weeks of July. We would then get a train to Victoria Station and from there get on a Birches Coach which would take us to Rushden Bus Station in Northampton. From there we would get another bus to Chelveston to stay with Granddad and Nanny Betts. Barry and I were not good travellers and suffered terribly from travel sickness. Mum or Dad used to have to get off the bus whilst either one of us was being sick. It plagued us throughout our childhood, until mum discovered that taking a tablet called Kwells would stop it. It was always that awful smell of diesel that would make me feel sick, and I tried as hard as I could not to think about it, but I always succumbed and had to tell mum that I really needed to get off the bus.

Meanwhile auntie Lil who had been expecting her first baby had given birth to a boy on 3rd January 1949 whom she called Eric. This meant Nan and Granddad now had 3 grandchildren and of course, being the eldest I felt quite important. I loved visiting auntie Lil and playing with my new baby cousin.

He was a rather sickly child who always had a runny nose and constantly had colds and chills but I was thrilled that there was a new baby for me to make a fuss of, although I don't think Barry cared one way or another.

Barry was happy in his own little world; wheeling his little wheelbarrow up and down the street and helping his friend Harry the street cleaner. By this time of course Barry was coming up to 5 years old and was due to start school that September. Mum had plans to return to work once Barry was at school. However like all best laid plans, there is always a hiccup, because about a couple of months after Eric was born, mum found out that she too was pregnant with her third child. From what she told me when I was older, she was not best pleased and she blamed my dad and wouldn't speak to him for a few weeks. When relating this to me in one of our chats years later laughingly I told her that it takes 'Two to tango'.

In February 1949 a month after Eric had been born, Dad's sister Jinny died of lung cancer. It was my first experience of death and on the day of the funeral, I had come home for lunch and mum had taken me round to my grandparents' house. The door of the Parlour was open and I peeked in. In front of the fireplace was my auntie's coffin which stood on two wooden trestles. All around the room were flowers from friends, neighbours and family and there was an awful smell about the room. I returned to school that afternoon but could not get the scene out of my mind and I ended up in tears. A kindly teacher took me to the headmistress and I was allowed to stay with her until it was time to go home.

During her pregnancy mum suffered problems with her teeth and in the end when she went to see a Dentist he told her that she had gum decease and there was no other option but to remove all her teeth. It had been caused through lack calcium during the war years and of course, she breast-fed Barry and me for many months, so no doubt we took a lot of the goodness from her body. Nowadays of course, they could probably have been saved. She had really beautiful white teeth that were all even, she must have been absolutely devastated at having to have them all removed. She was only 33 years old. She very soon got her dentures. Dad on the other hand had never had a good set of teeth so he decided that he would have his entire set of teeth out as well.

The day arrived when he too was to get his new dentures. He came home that evening and bounded up the stairs all excited anxious to show off his new teeth, as he came in the door with a big grin on his face, the top set of the denture slipped down. Mum, Barry and I just collapsed in giggles. Dad just looked so embarrassed. He did however return to the Dentist who adjusted them so that they would fit properly.

So on the 4th October 1949, another grandchild arrived my sister Veronica weighing in at a hefty 8lbs. Like Barry, mum had another home birth. I remember that day very well. Nan and picked us up from school that day and took us back to her house and given us our tea. She had explained to us on the way home that mum hadn't been very well that day so she had asked Nan to collect us from school. So we washed our hands and sat down to a meal with Nan and Granddad uncle Bill and auntie Lil. During the course of our meal, Nan said she had a surprise for us, wondering what this could be I thought perhaps it was a special cake she had made or something nice like that. Then she said that our mum was going to have a little brother or sister so that was why we were with them. Barry scowled and his immediate reaction was disgust to say the least and he said "Don't want a sister, they stink". As for me, I relished the idea of having a sister rather than another annoying brother.

After we had finished our meal sometime later Nan took us into the scullery and sat us both on the table and washed our faces and hands. She combed my hair and tied a red ribbon in it. Granddad said to Barry "Come here Dicky let's put some of Granddad's Brylcreem on to make you a smart boy". Barry's hair was combed flat and was shiny with the Brylcreem that granddad had rubbed into it. Then our Dad came in grinning all over his face "Has she had it Tom?" Nan enquired. "Yes Ivy's had a little girl weighing 8lbs". Nanny took hold of mine and Barry's hands and then proceeded to put our coats on and said "Come on we are going to see your little sister". Barry hung back, he was very annoyed and adamantly exclaimed "I told you I didn't want a sister take her back dad". Dad replied that he couldn't do that and he would soon come to love her.

So off we all went 5 doors away to see mum and the new baby. She was lying in bed in the front bedroom and in the crib by her side was our new little sister. She was adorable with a lot of black hair and tiny hands. I went up to her straight away and touched her little hand which coiled around my finger. Barry hung back, he just didn't want to see the new baby and of course, he was more than a little bit jealous as up to now he had been the baby. Mum coaxed him onto the bed and cuddled him and as she did so, he peeped out from under her arm and stole crafty look at his new sister. Gradually he got down from the bed and moved around to the crib and gently touched the baby's hand. He soon got over his jealousy and from that day on he loved her. "What are you going to call her" my Nan asked. "Veronica Mary" said mum; Mary is of course after you. Nan was so pleased, especially as my second name Ann had been after mum although she had shortened it to Ann rather than Annie and Barry's second name was Charles after our dad and granddad.

Word got around to the family in Northampton and to my uncle Bill who had married his wife Eva in 1941. This had been against my Nan Betts' wishes as Eva was about 5 years older than Bill, and because he was under the age of 21 Nan would not give her consent, so Bill had taken it to Court where permission was granted.

Much to his utter disappointment Bill and Eva had been unable to have children of their own so they were especially close to Barry and me. Bill came to see mum on his own as Eva was unable to travel. Mum had told Bill that she hadn't wanted another child and that she had been intending to go back to work. Bill said "My god Ivy, if you don't want such a beautiful baby I'll take her". Mum of course didn't really mean it, she was just hormonal.

As a family of 5 we were now officially over-crowded with only 3 rooms and a toilet. Dad had already written to the Council when they had found out that mum was expecting to see if we could be rehoused and after Veronica's birth he again contacted the housing department to advise them that she had been born.

About 3 weeks or so after the birth mum and dad got a letter to say they had been allocated a brand new flat in a housing development called Priory Court. They were the most up-to-date flats built since the war.

Mum and Dad left Barry, me and the new baby with our grandparents and went to the Town Hall to collect the keys to go and view the new flat.

The estate had gone up just after the war. The flats were in blocks and each block was given a letter of the alphabet, Blocks A, B, C, D and E and F had already been allocated and other blocks of flats were rapidly being built. Our flat was in Block 'L' and our new flat was on the third floor.

When mum and dad returned to our grandparent's house, they were full of news about the wonderful flat. Dad said that it had a separate bathroom with running water – no more bringing in the tin bath and filling it with water from the kettle and there was a separate toilet. It had three nice sized bedrooms; a large lounge and what's more, a fitted kitchen **WITH A FRIDGE**. They couldn't get over that. Fridges were an American idea; the only way Nan could keep her meat fresh was in the cold store which was built into the outside wall in the garden. I would imagine it was insulated in some way and had a metal cage around it.

This was the start of a new life for our family.

Uncle Ted, Nan Penn, Maureen and Barry in the garden at 20 Erskine Road.

2

² *Priory Court in the late 50s or early 60s D & E blocks*

CHAPTER SIX

1949 – 1952 – Moving and Growing-up

Mum and Dad got a moving date so they were kept busy wrapping and boxing up all their possessions. To make it a bit easier, one of Uncle Alf's friends had a market stall and said that Dad could borrow it to move some bits and pieces to the flat. The heavy stuff was to go in the removal van which they had booked from the only place they knew, yes – my old enemy **Mr.Dawson**. As it turned out they were an excellent firm and very professional.

Dad came home from work one day and fetched the stall and piled a lot of bits and pieces on to it. Uncle Ted came round to give him a hand and as a special treat I was allowed to go with them. Dad lifted me up and put me on top of the boxes. We progressed along Erskine Road, crossing over the road at the top and walking along the road opposite, until we came to the main Forest Road. We managed to negotiate this busy road and reached the other side. On the corner was a big Fire Station, and it was the road by the side of the Fire Station called South Countess Road that we had to negotiate. Unluckily for Dad and Uncle Ted, who were pulling and pushing the stall, it was quite a steep hill. We started to go down the hill ok, but as we got further down the stall gathered momentum, and poor dad and Ted were having a hell of a job holding it back. In the end, Dad lifted me down to make it a bit lighter and they managed to get to the bottom all in one piece.

Our block of flats was situated in the centre of the Priory Court Estate so dad and Uncle Ted pulled the stall along the road as it was easier and finally came to the block in question. Dad unloaded all the boxes with a little bit of help from me, and then put them in the lift and took them upstairs to the third floor to our flat, whilst Uncle Ted stayed downstairs with the stall. I have never been in a lift in my life and it was truly frightening, especially as I hated enclosed spaces, but Dad held my hand so I was ok.

The estate had only been partially built in 1949 – the building work had begun in 1946 or 1947 and the first few blocks had been constructed.

My first view of the flat was how nice and clean and modern it was. The front door opened up onto a fairly long hallway which was an 'L' shaped and to the right by the front door was another smaller hall with the toilet on the right and at the end was a modern bathroom. Just inside the front door on the right hand side at floor level was small door which opened up into a larger cupboard situated outside next to the front door. This was to accommodate the coal as of course we had to have the proverbial 'coal ole'. In those days there was no central heating and the flat was heated by a coal fire in the front room.

There were two doors leading off the hall on the left which were the 2 smaller bedrooms and at the top of the hallway was another door leading into the third bedroom – which would be my parent's room. Then just to the right of their bedroom door was the door leading to the lounge which was big compared to where we were living at that time. It was a rectangular shaped and had a window along the whole length of the room giving plenty of light. There were tiles on the floor which made it easy to clean. There was also a metal door with glass panels that led onto the balcony. Next to the lounge was the 'famous' fitted kitchen. It was painted in a pale grey colour and had nice tiles on the floor. On the left as you entered the kitchen was a big cupboard to store brooms, mops buckets and the like. There were cupboards all along the left side of the kitchen, and a small work top with a cupboard above with a set of drawers and a cupboard below. The worktop went back into a recess where there was a small hatchway with two doors that opened outwards into the lounge. There was another big larder type cupboard at the other end. At the end of the kitchen was another metal door with glass panels which also led out on to a quite a large balcony which had ample room for mum to put up a clothes line and hang out her washing. There was a chute on the wall which led down to a dustbin cupboard downstairs so all the rubbish would be thrown down the Chute and would automatically go into the big bins downstairs.

On the other side of the kitchen was the aluminium sink and draining board and room for a cooker, then in the corner dad showed me the fridge. Wow, I had never seen anything like it. It was on a raised plinth and situated under a counter so things could be stored on top. All in all I was very impressed.

When we went back downstairs I noticed a door leading off of the main entrance and asked dad where this led. He produced a key and unlocked the door and we went in. There were toilets to the side of the entrance and as we walked in there were separate little rooms each housing a washing machine and at the end room there were about 3 huge dryers for drying the washing. My Uncle Ted said what an improvement on where we had been living and at least mum had somewhere to do her washing and would not have to scrub it all by hand.

The last bits and pieces and been brought up to the flat and Dad showed Uncle Ted round and he commented how big it was.

Moving day soon arrived. Barry and I had to stay with our grandparents. The removal van came along from our favourite Removal firm – yes that's right **Dawsons**. Dad helped the men put all the furniture in the van then he went into the van with the removal men whilst mum put Veronica in the pram and we all walked round to the flat.

We settled in nicely and mum visited the schools in the area. I was enrolled in Blackhorse Road Junior School – I was coming up to 8 at the time and would have been in the junior school had I remained at Mission Grove. Barry was enrolled in the infants' school in St. Andrews Road.

We gradually got to know our neighbours. On the same landing opposite us were the 'Green' family, Bill and Vera Green and their two daughters Brenda and Angela. Brenda was a year younger than me and Angela a year younger than Barry. Brenda and I soon became friends. In the other side of the block on the same floor to us lived another family with whom we became friends they were the 'Wincklesses' They had three children, the eldest was Jean a year younger than me, Alan a year younger than Barry and June who was around the same age as Veronica. In the same block as the Wincklesses on the second floor on the opposite side and at the end of the block was another family called 'The Bucks'. They had a daughter Georgina who was 8 months younger than me and her brother Dennis who a year younger than Barry.

All of us us soon became firm friends and one day Jean and I and our brothers, Alan and Barry devised a system of communicating with each other. Their flat was in the other side of the block adjoining our flat; so it was a simple task to get a long double piece of string which I tied to the window lock on our window, I passed it over to Jean who then tied the other end to her window. Then we would each write a note and thread it through until it reached the other ones window. We used a peg to secure it onto the string. That is until my mum found it and made me take it down.

We used to play numerous games in and out of our blocks, including Hide 'n Seek, but the trick was to look at the reflection in the glass which surrounded the stair cases and the side entrances to the block. So all we had to do was to go out onto the grass and look up and we could see where the others were hiding by their reflections in the glass. We then ran to where the large dustbins were housed and shouted "Tin Pan Alley " and the name of whoever was hiding.

Barry at that time was keen on anything electrical and my mum's brother Bill had given him a Crystal set radio which he fiddled around with. One day he managed to get a wire out of his bedroom window and dropped it below – it was from a big reel of wire that Uncle Bill had given him, and he dragged the wire and fixed it to one of the new sapling trees at the back of the block which had been put in. The Crystal set worked a treat that is until my dad discovered it and made him dismantle it. Barry was always experimenting with items to do with wiring so it was really no surprise that ended up as an Engineer.

All our bread and was delivered by a Bakers Van which was pulled by a horse. As soon as they appeared in the road at the front all the children would go down to stroke him and feed him carrots, whilst our mums bought their loaves of bread.

Every Sunday the 'Fish Man' would push a little cart around where he had all kinds of seafood. Mum would buy this for our Sunday tea. We were particularly fond of winkles although I could never get the hang of teasing them out of their shells with a safety pin, but I used to get the 'eyes' and stick them on my face and pretend they were beauty spots like the film stars.

In the summer months the Ice Cream man would come round in his van – he was called 'Dicky Birds Ice-Cream' and there would be a chorus of "Mum – can I have an ice-cream?" If we were lucky, and our mum had a bit of spare cash, depending whether both Barry and I were shouting up, she would wrap a 3d bit or 6d bit in a bag and twist it round so that it didn't fall out and throw it off the balcony. Dicky Birds milky lollies were a particular favourite of all of us, but my favourite was Banana flavour.

A row of 4 shops had been built just along from our block which consisted of a small sweet shop a grocery shop, a butchers shop and a chemist. We used to love going in the sweet shop and buying sweet lollipops called "Dandy's" and they would last absolutely ages, and cost 3d bit. (1½p)

When we first moved to Priory Court Veronica was a baby in arms, and the following summer mum used to feed her and then put her in the pram and put her out on the grass downstairs to get the sun. Funnily enough Jean's mum did the same with baby June and other mothers followed suit. They kept an eye out for each other, particularly those who lived on the ground floor.

Brenda, Jean, Georgina and I got into many adventures. We would go to a sweet shop that was in Higham Hill called 'Chapples' where we would buy a packet of sweet cigarettes for 1d and pretend we were grown-ups smoking. Then of course we would devour them as they were quite tasty. We also bought penny badges from Chapples and took them home and painted initials on them **G.N.** which stood for 'Giant Nest Club'. This was a game we had invented where we would gather up the grass cuttings that the Council Workers had left and make a huge nest out of it. We would spend hours building it up, but of course it didn't last long because the Council would come along and take it away.

We found out that the air vents were hollow in the kitchen and when our parents were out; we would clamber up on to the draining boards and shout to each other through the air vents.

We had lived in Priory Court for about a year and a half when some enterprising person had thought up an idea of forming a Resident's Association. This person's name was Harry Pattle so he knocked on doors to see who would be interested and there was a good response to the idea. So the Association was set up. In order to raise money each block had a Representative who would collect money from all the members. My dad was one of the people who volunteered. The money would be placed in a Bank account and dances and other events were put on to increase the funds. Then when the time was ripe Mr.Pattle together with other members approached the Council to see if they would agree to build a Community Centre which would be attended by all the members. At a Council meeting the suggestion was put forward and passed.

By this time all the buildings had been completed and the surrounding areas were landscaped with grass the Court began to look quite nice. The Community Centre building was erected almost opposite to our block and adjoining this Council also built Tennis Court. Very soon dances were being held and the hall was let out for private functions to generate more funds. The Council charged a peppercorn rent to the Association.

The Residents' Association members organised a swimming club for the children in the Court. It cost us 3d each and we would all go to the swimming baths which at that time was at the top of Walthamstow Market. My first problem was that I didn't possess a swimming costume, so mum took out her sewing machine and she converted an old grey woollen swim suit that had belonged to her so that it fitted me. I cannot honestly say that I really enjoyed getting into the water, but I just used to stand in the shallow end. Then we would all get changed and go straight over to the Chippies opposite where we would buy a 3d bag of chips and eat them as we walked home again.

Later on the Tenants Association held dances in the Community Centre and we particularly liked the Old Time Dancing, such as the Gay Gordons and the Pally Glide. Brenda, Jean and I would turn up in long dresses. Mine were re-modelled from some old evening dressing given to me by my auntie Hetty, and mum being a clever needlewoman would take them apart and make them to fit me. I used to think I looked the *Bees knees"* in them when in actual fact, I must have looked rather strange in cut-down adults dress more like a 'little old lady cut down short', as my mum would say.

We had plenty of friends and I settled down nicely at school. I liked the school and was involved in a lot of activities and learned to play Netball and was in the team. The strangest thing was that I played in the position of Shooter but was the shortest in the team. I guess I could dodge around all the taller girls.

I joined the School Choir and my teacher told me that I had a 'pleasant' voice. Not content with just singing I also had a recorder which would drive my mum and dad up the wall with the horrible noise it made, but I thought it was lovely.

I had my second experience of death at the age of almost 9 years old, when on 21st October 1950 Granddad Penn passed away. He had been ill for quite some time, and had suffered from exposure to mustard gas during the WW1 and had also suffered quite badly from Asthma. He had died from a number of complaints including Asthma, heart problems, and chronic bronchitis. He was just 62 years old.

I was taken into the parlour where a few months earlier Auntie Jinny's coffin had lain to see Granddad's coffin. This time there was a huge wreath of Arum Lilies placed upon the coffin which gave off a very sweet heavy and sickly scent. Since that day, I have disliked Arum Lilies intensely as they remind me so much of Granddad's funeral. I think mum and dad left us children with a neighbour whilst they attended the funeral as of course, we were considered too young to attend.

When I was 10 I was old enough to go swimming with the school, so out would come the grey swim suit that mum had made. She bought me a rubber swimming hat as it was the rules that everyone had to have their head covered for health reasons. So off I went to my first swimming lesson. I had obviously been in a swimming pool before when I had belonged to the swimming club, so I looked forward to going with the school thinking that at least I might learn to swim. We were all taken to the shallow end and one by one we entered the water by going down the steps. The water was deeper than I anticipated and came up to my chest so I clung on to the rail around the edge of the pool. We did various exercises to get us used to the water and I didn't mind it at all. What I didn't like was when we got out of the water and it was freezing cold, and my grey woollen swim suit hung down all baggy where it was wet with the water. Of course this caused ridicule from the other kids and I ended up in tears.

However, I did persevere and in the end I persuaded mum to buy me a proper swim suit. I had been going swimming on probably 3 – 4 occasions and was getting used to being in the water, and even venturing away from the bar around the edge and standing up in the water. There were some boys who could swim and they were allowed to do their own thing whilst those of us who were non-swimmers just tried to learn. We had to lean forward and lift our legs off the floor so that we could float. I was getting there, then one day one of the boys who was a good swimmer thought it would be a lark to swim under the water and he came up to me and tugged on my legs and I immediately went under. The Lifeguard had seen this and dived in and brought me to the surface and got me out. I was terrified, the water had got into my lungs and I could not breathe. That did it for me; from that day on I have been scared of the water. Later on in life I did go to a Hypnotist and then took some swimming lessons and did manage to do a few strokes, but swimming is not and never will be one of my favourite pastimes.

Mum received a letter from Nan Betts to say that Auntie Rose was getting married on 10 February 1951 which would be her 21st birthday. This was another marriage that Nan had opposed but of course once Rose was 21 there was nothing that Nan could do about it. We were all invited and I was very excited about the prospect of going to a wedding.

Aunt Rose and Uncle Walt were to be married in the village church in Chelveston and the reception was being held in the church hall.

It was a bitterly cold day in February and we arrived at the church and sat down in the pews, heeding a warning from mum to be quiet. The vicar appeared and signalled the organist to begin playing the Wedding March and we all had to stand.

Auntie Rose looked lovely in a long white silk wedding dress with a small train. On her head she wore a full length veil that trailed behind her as she walked up the aisle on the arm of my proud granddad. Because of the cold weather she wore a little fur cape over her dress.

After the ceremony was over we all left the church to have the photographs taken. Rose had two bridesmaids who also wore fur capes over their dresses. The photographer obtained the photographs he wanted then we went on to the Church Hall where the wedding breakfast was set out.

After the meal the photographer was again present to take photos of Aunt Rose and Uncle Walt cutting the cake and then Nan asked if he would take a photograph of the whole family. So the photographer arranged some chairs with nan and granddad in the front with aunt Rose and uncle Walt and the rest of Rose's brothers and sisters sitting on chairs around them. I can't remember very much about that day only that it was cold.

In about April 1951 I began to feel very tired and lethargic and kept falling asleep. My mum put it down to always reading books but I was unwell with it. I just could not function. Nan Penn noticed this as she didn't see me quite as often as before, and she advised my mum to take me to see the doctor. Mum made an appointment and took me along to see the doctor. He examined me and said to mum that I was suffering from an illness called Glandular Fever and had to be hospitalised.

An ambulance was called and they came to our home. I was crying I didn't want to go to hospital, but I was so ill. I was taken to our local Whipps Cross Hospital and placed in a room on my own where the Doctor's diagnosis had been correct but they had also found that I had Catarrhal Jaundice coupled with an enlarged liver as well as Glandular Fever. Mum and dad would come to visit me with Barry but Veronica was too young so one day my Nan had come up with Mum and Dad and they brought Veronica. Then whilst Nan came in to visit, mum and dad stood outside my ward and lifted Veronica up so I could see her. They had brought lots of books for me to read and colouring books to keep me occupied, but I just wanted to get out of there. I was in a side ward so I didn't have anyone to talk to.

Then after about 2 weeks, I was moved to a general ward, and was surprised to find that my friend Georgina had been admitted. She had to have Polyps removed from her nose, she was only in hospital for a few days and I was sad when she went home whilst I remained there. After about 4 weeks I was discharged from hospital but was not allowed to go back to school. I had about 12 weeks off of school altogether so missed out on quite a bit of my education. In the summer of 1951 The Great Exhibition was held at Alexander Palace, but because I had been so ill, I was unable to go. Before I had become ill mum had planned to take me one day and dad would take Barry the next. So that was something else I had missed out on and of course, it was a 'one-off' and would never be staged again.

Whilst I had been in hospital a very nice chaplain and paid a visit and he bought me a Bible of my own. He had marked passages down for me to learn and always brought me new texts.

When I came out of hospital he visited me at home and coincidentally his surname was also PENN but he wasn't any relation to our family.

I got stronger and in September 1951 I returned to school. This would be my last year in the junior school and it was the year when we had to study in order to take our 11 plus the next year. I didn't do too badly in my course work, but having had so much time off the previous year I had a lot of catching up to do. Finally the 11 plus exams came around the following summer and I had to go to the Waltham Forest College which was in Forest Road in order to take the exams. I was extremely nervous about this and unsure as to what I was doing. Mum didn't help very much when I was getting ready to leave her comment was "I don't know why you are bothering to take these exams because I don't think you will pass".

She was right, my mind went completely blank with nerves and I did not do terribly well. Also the fact that I had lost so much schooling didn't help either.

A few weeks later we got the results, and whilst many of my classmates had passed, unfortunately I failed miserably. I suppose I was upset in a way, and quite envious of some of my classmates who were going on to Technical schools. I would be going up to Blackhorse Road Senior School for Girls.

My favourite pastime was reading. The school had an extensive Library and I joined the Library club. I would sit for hours and hours with my nose stuck in a book and really getting into the story so much so that very often I would not hear my mum talking to me.

Brenda, Jean, Gina and I formed a gang which we called 'The Black Hand Gang' god knows why we thought of that title, maybe it was because we were always mucky. As I was the eldest of the group I was made the 'Leader'. Barry sometimes joined in when I would let him. I was a tomboy in those days and would get more pleasure from playing football and cricket with Barry and his mates rather than taking part in 'girly' games such as playing with dolls. I think my mum despaired that I would ever grow up into a nice young lady.

At this time other blocks of flats had been completed and people were moving in and pretty soon we had another friend. Her name was Marion Proudfoot and she and her family – her mum Millie and dad Jack and older brother David – had moved into 'N' Block a few months before us. Jack was a Window Cleaner and acquired quite a reputation with the ladies. Marion told me that he used to take an empty bucket up to a customer and collect bets then taken them to a bookie as street betting was illegal in those days.

Marion was a vivacious girl and very popular and we became firm friends. So the five of us would go then around together.

In August 1951 mum received a telegram to say that Granddad Betts has passed away. Now I had lost two granddads in the space of just 10 months and in two years and experienced the deaths of three beloved members of my family. I came home from school to find mum crying and she told me that he had died on the 28th August. I was upset because I had loved my granddad, although I hadn't seen him very much since we had moved to Priory Court. He was just 61 years old and had died from coronary thrombosis and bronchitis. Dad got home and mum told him the news and arrangements had to be made for them to attend his funeral in Northampton where they still lived. Mum said that we would stay with our neighbour downstairs overnight whilst mum and dad would take Veronica with them and travel to Northampton for the funeral. They would stay with Nan Betts before coming home the next day.

It felt very strange sleeping downstairs and our neighbour, Mrs. Bartlett, made us a bread and butter pudding which Barry and I had never had before, but we ate it and it was quite nice

My sister was now a toddler and mum had finally got her way and had gone back to work. She had found a nice lady who lived in 'A' block who was a registered child minder so Veronica was left with her during the day whilst mum went to her job at a company of Dyers and Cleaners called the Tip-Top. The factory was one of many on an industrial estate in Sutherland Road Walthamstow. Mum worked as an Ironer. Larger items would be pressed, especially trousers. The press consisted of a long board covered in a cloth and above it was a lid which when pulled down on to the lower board, would emit steam which in turn would press the clothes. Mum would iron items such as shirts and skirts and then hang them on a rail where a lady would pin a label on them ready for collection by the customer. It was a tiring job as she was on her feet all day starting at 8 in the morning until 6 o'clock at night. I was around 11 years old at this time and I was given the task of collecting Veronica from the child minder when I came out of school and taking her home and looking after her until dad came in. Later on mum managed to get Veronica in a local nursery where she would take her in the morning before starting work and I would collect her again when I came out of school.

As I got older I would help with preparing the dinner ready for dad to finish when he arrived home from work and then we would all sit down and eat in our kitchen when mum got home. I didn't appreciate it then, but I realised how tired mum must have got because she still had household chores to do like washing and ironing. I must admit I used to moan when I was asked to help as being the eldest daughter I was told it was my duty. Mum did teach me how to iron handkerchiefs and pillow cases which I was allowed to do on a Sunday night to give her a rest. There was always a play on the radio Sunday evening which I loved to listen to so I would take my time ironing the hankies and pillowcases so that I could stay up longer and listen to the play.

Mum began to suffer from pains in the calves of her legs probably caused by standing all day. She visited the doctor who told her that the arteries in her legs were blocked and he told her that to alleviate the pain she should lose weight and give up smoking. Mum had never been a slim woman, and after having each of us three children, she had put on more weight. My Nan Betts was also a big lady and mum used to say that she had inherited it from her own mother. She had never smoked when she had first got married but she told me that it was when she was pregnant with me one of her work mates had persuaded her to try a cigarette saying it would calm her nerves. As it was during the war I guess it made sense at the time. From then on she became addicted and smoked quite heavily during her lifetime.

Mum made a few friends and she met my future husband's mother and his sisters who all worked at the Cleaners. The women formed a darts team and joined darts League Called the Social League which was an amalgamation of firms in the area. Mum was quite a good darts player and so was *'Moll'* (my future mother-on-law), but that is another story for later on in this book. Between them they won a few trophies and it did my mum good to get out now and again and meet other people socially.

Now and again the Community Centre would lay on special party nights which mum and dad attended with their friends Rose and Jack Rhodes who lived on the ground floor. I used to be quite envious of them going out and wished that I was older enough to accompany then

When we had lived at Erskine Road, Mum would get all her groceries from a shop called the United Dairies in the High Street, I think that is where her Ration books were registered for groceries such as tea, butter milk, cheese and eggs etc., so when we moved to Priory Court she continued to get her main shopping from there. As I got older I was given the money with a shopping list and when I got home from school I had to put Veronica in the pram and take her with me to do the shopping.

Mum would always put chocolate biscuits on the list and ordinary biscuits, and by the time I got home, there were a few chocolate biscuits missing. I consider that to be my perk for doing the shopping.

One evening I collected Veronica from the Nursery as usual, but this time I left her and Barry at our neighbour's house. Then I got the pram out of the shed and taking the money and the shopping list walked to the Market to get the shopping.

It took me about 25 minutes or so to walk to the shop. When I arrived, I handed the list to the assistant, who by this time knew who I was and passed some pleasantries with me as she collected all the items together that were on mum's list. She then put them into shopping bags for me and I put them into the pram and made my way home.

By this time it was getting dark as I think it was around October time of the year. I had got about half way up Erskine Road when I heard footsteps behind me. I moved to one side to allow the person to pass by, but to my surprise it was a man and he caught me up and kept in step with me as I walked along.

He began to try to make conversation with me asking me my name and where I was going. Mindful of my earlier experience when I was younger I kept going and didn't reply. "Surely you can tell me your name young lady" he said. I didn't reply "Have you got a baby in that pram?" He asked. I said "No – go away and leave me alone". "Well if you want a baby, I can give you one" he said threateningly. I was panic stricken and realised the danger I was in so I pushed the pram a little bit faster and luckily a lady was coming towards us so I shouted out to her "Please help me this man won't leave me alone". As soon as I did that the man turned round and began walking in the opposite direction. "Are you ok dear?" the lady asked. By this time I was in tears and very frightened. So she asked me where I lived and I told her, she immediately turned round and walked with me until I reached home. She asked if I would be ok now and I said yes. I managed to get the shopping upstairs but at first I was too scared to tell my dad what had happened in case he blamed me for being over-friendly. However later in the evening I did tell mum and dad what had happened and to my surprise they didn't tell me off. After that incident, mum and dad had obviously decided that perhaps it wasn't sensible to send me such a long way especially when it was dark. When I think back to then and nowadays, I don't think any parent in their right mind would let their child, especially a ten or eleven-year old go that far on their own.

If mum ran out of anything at the weekend she would send me round to a corner shop called Mills which was on the corner of Luton Road and Winns Avenue where they sold everything. It was run by a mother and her two sons, one of whom had a hare lip, and being children we would be fascinated by the way he spoke. Mills sold fresh bread and whenever mum sent me to get a loaf; I would pinch out the end of the loaf and eat it on the way home. I always got told off, but that didn't stop me and the smell of new baked bread was so tempting. On the other corner were the Greengrocers called Con Woods and they would open for a few hours on a Sunday morning just selling vegetables.

One particular day mum had sent me round to get some potatoes from Con Woods and afterwards to pop into Mills to get some other groceries and her cigarettes. On the way home I met one of my friends so we chatted and walked along with me swinging the shopping bag. When I got home, mum emptied the bag and then said "Maureen where's my ciggies?" I shrugged and said "I don't know Mr.Mills put them in the bag for me". Then she discovered a small hole in the bottom of the bag through which the cigarettes had probably fallen out. Boy did I get it in the ear then, she was absolutely furious. I did offer to walk back to see if I could find them but she said "Oh somebody has probably picked them up by now, you stupid girl, when will you ever learn, you spend half of your time in a daydream instead of concentrating on what you are doing". I was so upset and ended up in tears and was very sorry I had incurred my mum's anger. She did have a temper and when she was riled, then you had to get out of the way. I must admit I have inherited a temper from her and when they were small my two sons made quick exits if I was on the warpath.

Many events were held in the community hall in order to generate more funds and help run the club a nominal entrance fee would be charged to go towards to upkeep and of course to go towards the rent for the Centre.

A Youth Club was formed although at the time I was too young to belong to this. They would hold fetes in the summer which always drew large crowds.

In February 1952 King George the VI died and Elizabeth II came to the throne. The Coronation was planned for June 2nd 1953 and The Priory Court Residents Association decided to hold a fete with a fancy dress. My mum was kept very busy with her sewing machine making outfits for us kids. I was to go as a Hula Hula girl. She made me a grass skirt from raffia stitched on to a band of material. Then she made me a bra of the same material as the band and a wreath of flowers for my hair made from coloured crepe paper. Barry went as a pirate with a rakish three-corner hat on his head and a black patch over one eye. He wore a white shirt which mum had altered from one of his old school shirts. She had removed the collar stitched the edge down and had also made him a pair of black pantaloons. Around his waist he wore a blue sash. Veronica went as a Jester. She had a hat made of striped material which fitted close to her head, with three protruding horns coming out of the top. The remainder of the costume was made from the same material which was an all-in-one and on her feet she had ballerina slippers with coloured pom-poms sewn on the front. She was only three and half years old, and looked really cute in the outfit.

All the children were made to parade around the field and judges looked at each age group and the best costume won a prize. I felt so grown up especially as I had a bra on although I didn't have much to put in it at that time since I was only eleven and a half. Unfortunately because of the lack of 'boobs' as I paraded round feeling like the *Bees knees'* my bra began to slip down. I quickly hitched it up and went red with embarrassment. I don't know whether or not anybody noticed it, but I certainly did. I didn't come anywhere in the fancy dress, but Barry won second prize and Veronica won first prize. We did however all receive token Coronation mugs and saucers. I think I still have my mug somewhere.

There were all kinds of stalls, such as tombola, hoopla where you had to throw a ring to land over a prize, and a game where people had to guess how many beans there were in a jar, also they had to guess the weight of a cake, it was all good fun and everyone joined in. All the stalls were run by volunteers. In the evening there was a big party in the community hall, which was a lovely end to what had been a very successful day.

The Council had made provision for allotments at the rear of some of the blocks of flats, some of which were at the rear of 'L' Block. Dad, being a keen gardener applied and got one them which was a corner plot. I used to help him weed it and sometimes he would let me plant the seeds. We kept all the gardening tools in the pram shed which was downstairs at the back of the block of flats. Dad has previously had another allotment although I cannot remember where this was, but I do recall mum and dad taking us all there one summer where we had a picnic. I seemed to remember it was near some reservoirs somewhere.

Looking back to those days it seemed that the summers were long and hot and we played out until late at night when it was still light at 10 o'clock. I was not allowed to go far and could play out as long as mum and dad could see me from the balcony.

During the day of course mum and dad were at work and I had to look after Barry and Veronica. One Christmas Barry and Veronica had both received bikes, I think they were both second-hand but dad had done them up. I too had asked for a bike but was told "No you are too scatty to have a bike, you would probably have an accident on one" which I thought was so unfair. Once again I defied my parents, and got the key to the bike shed, and took my dad's bike and rode it around Priory Court. Of course it was miles too big for me and I couldn't reach the pedal sitting on the saddle so would put my legs through the cross bar and ride it without sitting down. I am pleased to say that I never ever got caught as I was very careful to be out of sight of our flat

One day I was playing out as usual with Brenda, Jean, Marion and Gina. Gina's parents had bought her a bike for her birthday and I was so envious. I asked her if I could have a go but she refused but then said she would give me a 'saddler' that is she would ride the bike standing up and I could sit on the saddle. Well I agreed anything to get on the bike. Gina was peddling furiously taking us both round the block but unfortunately she turned rather quickly resulting in both of us falling off, but somehow as we came off the bike the brake handle dug into inside of my arm resulting in a rather nasty gash that would not stop bleeding. So I had to go upstairs to get it seen to by my mum. She cleaned it all up and of course I

106

had to admit how the accident had occurred. Once again I got a good telling off. The cut was very deep and quite honestly I should have gone to the hospital and had it stitched but mum patched me up and put a bandage on my arm then I promptly went out to play once again with a warning from mum ringing in my ears 'Don't get on the bike again'. I still have the scar to this day.

Veronica's bike was a little three wheeler and Barry had a small two wheeler bike. He would go off with his friends from downstairs but I was stuck with Veronica. All the people in the block loved her because she was so cute when she was small, and the man on the ground floor would call her *'Babe'* so from then on that is what everyone called her. However, when she began to speak we tried to get her to say her name, but she couldn't quite manage 'Veronica' instead it came out as 'Wonkika' which was very quickly shortened by Barry and me to 'Wonki'.

One summer when we were off from school, Brenda, Jean and Georgina said that they were going to go on a picnic the next day to Epping Forest and asked if I wanted to come. I said yes, but would ask my mum and dad first. So when they got in from work that night I asked them if I could go. Their immediate answer was an emphatic 'NO' I think at that time Veronica was probably at the nursery. I only know that it was me and Barry, so I had to look after him.

I was determined not to be left out, so despite what my parents had said and I was a defiant little madam, I decided that I would go with my friends for a picnic in Epping Forest. So the next day dad had gone to work and mum dropped Veronica off at the Nursey on her way to work. The coast was clear so I got an old bottle and filled it up with tap water. I got the bread out of the cupboard and put butter and jam on four slices and cut them and wrapped them up in some paper, then got a carrier bag out of the cupboard and put the water and the sandwiches in it. Barry was a bit reluctant to go but I said that we were going and that was that.

We met the others downstairs and off we went. I am not certain how we got there I think we must have walked because I don't think any of us had any money. We finally arrived at a place with a pond which was called The Rising Sun. The pond had been caused by a bomb crater and had filled up with water over the years; it was named after a Pub that stood nearby. It was a lovely warm sunny day and there were lot of children with their parents playing on the grass. Brenda and Jean said they were going for a paddle and had brought a jam jar with them and said they were going to try to catch some tadpoles. I of course went with them and Barry tagged along. We were having fun and Jean had caught something in the jar, I don't know what it was, Barry stepped forward to look the next minute he had tripped and landed head first in the water. Luckily a lady nearby had seen what had happened and she quickly ran into the water and pulled him out. He was soaked from head to foot. The lady who was with some children of her own, got a towel and dried him off as best as she could.

I knew that I was in dead trouble now. I took Barry's shirt off and tried to dry it as much as I could by spreading it over a bush. It did dry to some extent but was absolutely filthy. It was time to make our way home, so I put the shirt back on him and off we went.

We got in before mum and dad got back from work so I told Barry to change his clothes and put the dirty ones in the washing basket and mum would be none the wiser. Huh famous last words! Unknown to me, Brenda had told her mum what had happened so as soon as mum came in from work Mrs. Green was knocking on the door and related the events to her; with the effect that when Mrs. Green had gone back indoors, I was in for the high jump. I was told that as I was the eldest I should have known better, and what had she and dad told me the night before that I was not allowed to go to Epping Forest. My mum once again came out with her now famous words "You just wait until your father gets home". Sure enough as soon as dad walked in the door mum was yapping away telling him what I had been up to, so out came the cane from the broom cupboard and then three whacks across my legs leaving nasty red wheals. I stayed in my bedroom crying and as a further punishment was not allowed any tea. Although my mum relented later in the evening after she had calmed down and did bring me a sandwich.

It was not the first time I had had this punishment either. Whenever I did anything wrong my mum would threaten me with "You wait until your dad gets home". Invariably as soon as he walked in the door mum would be telling him of my misdeeds and I would be taken into my bedroom where I would receive 2 or 3 whacks across the legs with the bamboo cane.

I must admit I was rather a defiant little girl, and very stubborn to boot. One day when I had yet again been punished; I waited until everyone was in the front room and crept into the kitchen, I opened the broom cupboard and took hold of the cane and went out onto the balcony. I opened the chute door and threw the cane down the chute. I was quite triumphant and marched into the lounge and announced that my dad couldn't hit me anymore with the cane because I had gotten rid of it. Silly me! I thought I was being so clever, but my dad was even cleverer than me, because he did no more than grab hold of me and march me downstairs and made me get inside this horrible smelly bin and retrieve the cane. So I got another wack for my trouble. Did I learn from this – well not really, it must have been something in my makeup because I knew I was doing wrong but it didn't stop me.

There were a few more times that I received this punishment, but my brother and sister always got away with it because in their words my parents said "You are the eldest so should set an example". Looking back either I was stupid or had a death wish, because no matter how much I was punished I never seemed to learn my lesson. I think I was jealous of my younger siblings; they seemed to get more attention than me so by being naughty I got the attention I wanted, although obviously not the right kind.

One Christmas time Barry and Veronica persuaded me to climb up to the cupboard in Mum and Dad's room where we knew they had hidden our Christmas presents. Like an idiot I did climb up on top of Dad's tallboy and opened the cupboard and sure enough there they all were all nicely wrapped. I climbed down again and said that there were all there. What did Barry do, as soon as my dad got home from work he said in a whining voice "Daaad, guess what Maureen done today, she climbed up your tallboy and saw our Christmas presents". Out came the cane and I got three swift stripes across the leg while Barry sniggered. Don't worry, I got him later and slapped him. Then of course I got into trouble again because I had hit him. Oh why didn't I learn?

Don't get me wrong, my parents were not cruel people, I guess that was how they had been disciplined and it carried on with their own children, or at least with me. I vowed that when I had children I would never ever hit them. I believed there were ways to make your children obedient without the need to hit them. I can honestly say that when I did become a mum I never smacked my sons, but instead withdrew privileges that hurt them much more than if I had smacked them.

In order to earn extra money my mum took in a variety of homework jobs. One of them was making tassels to go onto cushion covers, another was assembling toys, and then she got the best job of all from a local firm called Britain's who actually made toy soldiers. I think everyone worked for this company at one time or another. She would get a batch of toys and was instructed on the colours in which they had to be painted. She was provided with the paint in the form of powder to which she had to add water.

I was about 11 years old at that time, and was still into reading and would enter into a fantasy land being one with the story. I was reading one particular story in which the heroine was a beautiful girl with long golden hair. I was quite a plain little girl with light mousy hair and plumpish and I had always imagined myself to have golden hair and be beautiful like my heroine.

I had come home from school at lunchtime; mum and dad were at work so I made myself and Barry some lunch. Then I hit on an idea. I went into the living room where mum had all her homework stashed and found some gold paint. I mixed some of the powder with water and then I wet my hair and poured the whole of the concoction over my head thinking now I would have lovely gold hair. Unfortunately my hair didn't dry out so I had to take the afternoon off from school.

By the time mum came home that evening my hair had dried into a yellow sticky mess. Barry split on me and told mum what I had done. She got hold of me and took me into the bathroom and after several washes the paint finally came out of my hair.

I didn't get the cane this time as I was getting older so mum and dad probably thought that it was useless punishing me with it. Instead as a punishment I was not allowed to go on the school outing to London Zoo, which was due to take place the following week. That really upset me I begged and begged to be allowed to go but they stood firm. That hurt me more than any caning I had received. Mum had to write to the school and explain what I had done, so I then got a second telling off from the headmistress. Whilst my friends enjoyed their day out I was made to sit in the classroom doing arithmetic which by the way, I absolutely hated. Lesson learned I think!

One of the Blocks in Priory Court
Mum standing on our balcony in Priory Court

CHAPTER SEVEN

1955 – 1956 – Teenage years

I was coming up to 13 and had started to notice boys. I had a friend at school called Carole Bush. She was boy-mad and very popular with the boys. Her mum indulged her and was always buying her nice clothes. I was quite envious of her. She was always making fun of me and showing off in front of the other kids. I used to laugh it off, until one day I snapped. She had been saying something derogatory to me on the way home from school, I just got hold of her by her long hair and swung her around. We ended up in a fight and this time, I was the victor. She didn't speak to me for a long time afterwards, but neither did she take the mickey.

I was allowed to join the Youth Club together with Brenda, Jean, Georgina and Marion. We would listen to records, and play table tennis and other games. I really felt grown up and looked forward to Thursday evenings. By this time Jean and Brenda and paired up and Marion, Georgina and I were quite good friends. Georgina didn't always hang around with us, but Marion and I were mates. Of course I had started to notice boys as well; there was one particular boy who was a lot older than us who would come to the club. His name was Micky Finn; I believe he was of Irish descent. He would stroll in like he owned the joint dressed in a black overcoat. His hair was smarmed back with Brylcreem and behind him was his two mates – looking every bit like his body guards. He was very good looking as a lot of Irish boys are and of course he would have the girls swarming around him. I admired him from afar I wouldn't give him the satisfaction of being one of his 'groupies'. I think he ended up in prison or dying young so I heard on the grapevine many years later.

Of course there was another crowd of boys whom we used to hang around with and they were a lot older. One night they produced a pack of cigarettes and offered them around to Marion, Georgina and myself. Georgina was the first to try one and she coughed and spluttered so much that I said to myself *'I'm not going to look an idiot and make a fool of myself'* So I declined and I thank god I did and to this day I have never ever smoked.

Marion was the youngest in her family, her brother David was about 5 years older than she was and was already working. He was quite a good looking boy and he had his pick of girls. Marion was a fun girl to be with, in some ways she was older than her years. She always seemed to wear nice clothes and was very popular with the boys. I would often ask my mum to buy me a new skirt or blouse but she would often say she couldn't afford it. I would then say that Marion's mum had bought her this or that and mum's reply would be "I have got 3 children to clothe and feed Marion's mum has only got her".

She always had an answer to everything. Mum used to buy our shoes from a Tally Man called Mr.Cowell who would come round the door. He had an office at the top of his house which was in Wadham Road, Walthamstow. It was all up hill and quite a long way. As it was not on a bus route, I had to walk and it was quite a long trek. I would sometimes be sent to his house to get some shoes and would be taken up to this little room where there were racks and racks of boxes containing shoes. I would be told how much I could spend and would love going up there and trying them all on. Mum would then pay weekly for the shoes. She would also buy our clothes and pay weekly for them too. Sometimes if she was really hard up, she would visit 'Annie's' which was a second hand shop in Linton Road (just off the High Street with the jewellers Fish Brothers on the corner). Mum was very familiar with this particular jewellers because when she ran short of money she would visit the Pawnbrokers in Linton Road or 'Uncles' as it was known then and pawn her engagement ring.

Inside Annie's' there would be racks of clothes around the shop and in the middle a big pile of shoes which we would sort out. A lot of families in those days would visit 'Annie's as she was quite well known and as previously mentioned, mum was good with her sewing needle, she would alter the clothes to fit me and my brother and sister.

Another trend in those days was to wear bright fluorescent socks in pink, green or orange with ballerina shoes. Looking back now they must have looked horrendous but we all thought we looked good. I wore those Ballerina shoes all the time, and they wore out pretty quickly. As they were only cheap mum would give me the money to go to the Market and get new ones.

Sometimes dad would repair our shoes on the cobblers' Last that he had inherited from my Granddad Betts. However, Mum did have her moments of generosity, our neighbour on the ground floor had a sister called Iris who was a dance teacher and she offered to start up a dance club teaching us Tap dancing and this was held in the laundry room which was beneath the block. It would cost us 6d (2½p) each week. Mum agreed to let me go. So Brenda, Jean Marion and Georgina and a few others joined and we were taught to tap dance by this lady. Of course none of us had proper tap shoes, but as the weeks went by one by one their mothers bought tap shoes for the other girls, I was the exception and I felt totally left out. In the end mum gave in and once again I paid Mr.Cowell a visit and was shown a gorgeous pair of Red tap shoes. I really felt the *'Bees-knees'* in them and at last I could tap dance properly. Iris promised us that we would put on a show but after about a year some of the girls lost interest and the club folded up. Mind you when I considered how hollow the laundry rooms were it must have sounded horrendous to those residents on the first floor as we all practised our tap dancing and the noise of many tapping feet reverberated all around.

As to my tap shoes, I ended up wearing them for school when my other shoes had worn out. Dad had taken the taps off, but because they only had thin soles they wore out very quickly and in no time at all I had a hole in the sole. Mum would cut out a sole from a cornflake box and put them inside my shoes, and that would last a while that is until it rained and the cardboard sole would very quickly become sodden. Of course kids in my class soon realised that my family did not have much money and one girl, whose parents were quite well off even offered to give me her old shoes. However, after a visit to Annie I procured a second hand pair of shoes which I had to make do with.

My earlier problem with my waterworks still persisted and I was still finding it very hard to hold myself. There was one particular incident I recall when we had a school concert. We were all sitting in rows around the school hall when I badly wanted to go to the toilet. I put my hand up and asked the teacher sitting near us if I could be excused; she said no I had to wait. I couldn't of course. As much as I crossed my legs and went red trying to hold back very soon I felt the hot trickle of wee running down my leg into a puddle on the floor. The teacher spotted this and took me out of the hall. "Why didn't you go to the toilet before the concert?" she asked I told her that I did but I had problems. She was very cross and I had to get a mop and clean it up afterwards. Of course there was a lot of sniggering going on and name calling like "Old pen nibs wet-drawers". I should add that my surname was PENN so of course I was often called by different names like *'Pen and ink, pen nibs'* and so on.

After this incident the school contacted my mother and she was then forced to do something about it. She took me to the doctor and I was referred to Whipps Cross Hospital. A short time later, I was admitted for a bladder-stretching operation and was in hospital for about a week. When I returned to School I was under strict instructions that I had to use the toilet every half an hour for a few days, and then gradually stretch it out to three quarters of an hour then an hour. The hospital had provided mum with a letter which she took to the headmistress. I wouldn't say it cured me completely but it was a lot better after that.

In September 1953 I started at the Senior School and was placed in year 1A in a Miss Endecott's class. There were a few girls from the junior school so I was not without friends. Miss Endecott taught English which I very much enjoyed and found that I was quite good at this subject. Every week we would be given 10 new words which we had to learn and then on Friday afternoon would be tested on the spelling. My spelling was good and I received good marks. I also enjoyed Literature hearing about various authors and poets. I did not take very well to Shakespeare and found his works to be quite boring. I expect it was the old language that made it so.

I did enjoy life at the senior school and got on quite well. I particularly liked music and joined the Choir. History was another favourite subject as I loved hearing about the Kings and Queens of long ago, and also how the common folk lived. I still have that interest to this present day.

Art was another favourite subject of mine and I excelled at this; especially when we were taught how to make papier-mâché models by soaking newspapers and then forming them around a ball and shaping them. Then when it was dry we were allowed to decorate and paint the model. We were also taught perspective and how to draw objects near to and far away.

There was a boy who had moved into the other side of our Block whom I was particularly keen on and his name was Chris Tilling. He was a couple of years older than me and I thought he was so good-looking. We had our usual crowd which included Marion and me and occasionally Brenda and Jean and Chris began hanging out with us too. Before too long we were girlfriend and boyfriend and would talk about when we got older we would get married and have four children. I really did like him, but I don't think his mother liked me very much; she was a bit of a snob. Chris had an older sister called Jean who was going out with a boy in the Army. Then all of a sudden there was an announcement in the local Guardian that she had got married when her boyfriend had come home on leave. I don't know if the reason for the quick marriage was that she was pregnant, but it did seem rather sudden.

Soon after that Chris began going out with some mates and he joined the Army cadets so I saw less and less of him. By this time we both had other interests, and I had met other boys in the crowd who caught my eye.

Although I was growing up fast, I still remained a bit of a tomboy and would borrow my Brother Barry's skates and whiz around Priory Court with my friends. One day we were all chatting standing beneath the block and I was leaning against the big glass window and as I straightened up the skates rolled forward and my elbow banged against the window rather hard and a large crack appeared in it. We all made a hasty retreat and I never owned up to the damage.

All of dad's family were Tory supporters and as such they all belonged to the Conservative club which at that time, was situated at the top of Walthamstow Market. Dad was definitely the rebel; he was the only one to support Labour – perhaps I inherited my wilfulness from him who knows?

In 1954 when having a night out at the Conservative Club, Uncle Ted introduced Uncle Alf to a lady friend of his called Iris, the result was that Uncle Alf began courting her. She was a really nice lady, and very well spoken (or as we termed it at the time, 'very posh'). Iris was always dressed nicely, and had a good job in the city as a Shorthand Secretary. She later helped me a lot with my shorthand and gave me some of her old Shorthand exercise books which I have kept to this day. I believe her father was a Director of a Company. Iris lived with her parents in Northcote Road in a very large house. Also living with them was her Cousin Annie, and Iris's younger sister.

Alf and Iris fell in love and decided to get married. My Nan breathed a sigh of relief as Alf was now in his mid-thirties and Nan, and indeed all of the family, were beginning to think he would never get spliced. To my great joy, Iris asked me and Veronica to be her bridesmaids and Eric to be a pageboy. It was a dream comes true, especially as I had missed out on being a bridesmaid at the proposed wedding of Uncle Ted when I was younger.

Soon we were going for fittings as Iris had the dresses made specially. Mine was a long pale blue taffeta dress with a sweetheart neckline and short sleeves. It was fitted in at the waist and flared out into a long full skirt. My headdress was made of pale blue feathers which fitted close to my head and matched the colour of the dress. Veronica's dress was in a white flocked material with a round frilled neckline. It had short frilly sleeves and she wore a white satin sash around her waist. On her head she wore a Dutch bonnet tied with a white satin ribbon. Her dress was also full length. Eric was dressed in a frilly white satin shirt and pale blue taffeta trousers.

The date was fixed for 21st August 1955 – the day before mum and Dad's 19th Wedding anniversary. My Uncles Alf and Ted and the bride's father were all dressed in top hat and tails - it was a very posh wedding. They were married in St. Michaels and All Angels in Palmerston Road Walthamstow. Veronica and I carried bouquets of pink roses and summer flowers, and we both wore gloves to match our dresses. Iris had a teardrop-shaped bouquet of the same flowers, and wore a full length lace wedding gown with a high collar and long sleeves. Her headdress was made like a crown of flowers attached to which was an elbow length veil. She looked lovely.

Afterward the wedding ceremony we had photos taken then were driven to the reception which was held in a Hotel in Woodford. I absolutely lapped up the experience of being driven in a posh Limo. It was a lovely warm sunny day and after the reception we all gathered in the lovely grounds of the hotel to have more photographs taken. By this time I was nearly 14 years old and had begun to develop a figure. I felt so grown up in my dress, and I didn't want the day to end. Iris and Alf went off on their honeymoon and we all returned to Nan and Granddads house to continue the celebrations.

It was around the late 50s that Nan's house was compulsorily purchased by the Council and of course Nan and Uncle Ted, Uncle Bill, Auntie Lil and Eric had to move out. The Council moved them into brand new flats that had been built in Prospect Hill Walthamstow. Nan and

Uncle Ted had a nice ground floor flat with two bedrooms and Uncle Bill, Auntie Lil and Eric were housed in a 2-bedroom second floor flat which led off of a communal balcony.

Mum and Dad would often take us to visit Nan and she seemed quite happy. Before they moved out of their old house, their old faithful dog Peggy had died with old age, and Uncle Ted buried her in their back garden. The strangest thing happened, a year after Peggy died a Lilly appeared on the spot where she was buried in the garden but it was no ordinary lily, it was black one (or at least a very dark purple). Uncle Ted swore that he had never planted any lilies, let alone in that part of the garden. About a year after they moved into the new flat, Uncle Ted came home with a little spaniel puppy bitch which Nan called Sally. She was gorgeous and Nan spoilt her rotten as did Uncle Ted. Unfortunately as Sally got older she became quite boisterous and also being a bitch she really should have been spayed or even had been allowed to have at least one litter of puppies. She also became very jealous of Nan as she was Uncle Ted's dog to all intents and purposes because he made such a fuss of her.

Then one day Sally jumped up at Nan and knocked her flying, and as she was such a little woman it quite frightened her. So eventually Uncle Ted had to get rid of her. He could not find anyone to have her, even though I pleaded with mum and dad to let us have Sally, but of course that was impossible living in an upstairs flat as we did at the time. So Sally was put to sleep, and I was so upset over that.

I was a dog-lover right from my younger days when I would play with Peggy and dad told me that the family were never without a dog. I pleaded with mum and dad to have a pet, and later on they did buy us a budgie, although it was not the same as having a dog.

We all loved our budgie and we named him *'Butch'*. He had a light blue breast and white plumage and being a cock bird he soon learned to talk. He was very tame and when he was let out of his cage, he would immediately fly to one of us and perch on our shoulders. Unfortunately one day during the summer holidays I had gone indoors to get something and of course, Butch was out of his cage. He flew on to my shoulder and not thinking I had gone out again, forgetting he was still sitting on my shoulder; with the result that he had flown off and we never saw him again. I was distraught and it didn't help when mum and dad remonstrated with me for being so careless. Needless to say, we never got another budgie.

One summer's day I had been to our local Lloyds Park and on the way home I saw a stray dog, at least I thought it was a stray and it began to follow me. I encouraged it and it followed me all the way home, so I took it up to the flat and when mum opened the door the dog walked in. "What an earth have you brought home now?" She asked. So I told her that it didn't have a home and had followed me so I assumed that I could keep it. Mum told me in no uncertain terms to take the dog back where I had found it she said "Someone is probably looking for the dog and is upset, how you would feel?" So reluctantly I called the dog that followed me obediently and I retraced my steps to where I had found him. There was a lady standing at the gate of one of the houses looking up and down the road, and when she spotted me with the dog in tow, she came running up to me "Oh you have found him he got out thank you dear". Then turning to the dog she scolded him and quickly took him back to her house. So mum was right after all.

There was another time, when I found a small bird that appeared to have an injured wing. I picked it up and took it home, and found an old shoe box lined it with newspaper and some cotton wool I had found in the bathroom cabinet and laid it in the box. I looked after that little bird for days but unfortunately it died so my friends and I had a burial ceremony downstairs on dad's allotment. I didn't tell him that was where I had buried it.

My Auntie Hettie would visit Nan every week and she would wash her curtains, clean her windows and do bits of housework as by now Nan was getting older and was unable to do these things for herself. Her flat was immaculate as Uncle Ted also used to clean every weekend when he was home. Nan would also look forward to her two weeks holiday either in Yarmouth, Margate or Isle of Wight. She would go away with Uncle Ted, Auntie Hettie and Uncle Arthur, and occasionally Uncle Alf would go too before he met Iris and I believe that they went on one or two occasions after they were married.

A year or so after the wedding Auntie Iris fell pregnant, but sad to say her little girl was stillborn. I just cannot imagine how traumatic that must be to carry a child for 9 months and then for the baby to be born dead.

Alf had bought a brand new house in Chigwell and had opened up a Tyre fitting business in Walthamstow. Auntie Iris had given up her job to help Uncle Alf and she would do all the accounts. In fact she was the brain behind the business.

The house in Chigwell had 4 bedrooms and a nice lounge. There was a fitted kitchen and a remarkable gadget for those times which was a waste disposal unit in the sink which meant you could throw food waste in the sink and it would reduce it to mush and send it down the drain. There was also a separate dining room which was quite spacious. We visited the house shortly after they moved in and I loved it and where it was located, not far from the forest. Dad of course, was a bit scathing about

Uncle Alf buying the house as he was the first one in the family to do so. Dad's remarks were "Oh getting a mortgage is like having a millstone around your neck". I of course disagreed with this and said that I would love to own my own house one day.

Auntie Hettie, Uncle Ted and Nanny Penn in Yarmouth

Uncle Alf & Aunt Iris's wedding 21stAugust 1955.
In the picture above l to r:
Nanny Penn, Uncle Ted, Sister Veronica Aged 5 years 10
months Uncle Alf Auntie Iris Cousin Eric aged 6 years 7
months Aunt Iris's mother, me – aged 13 years 9 months
Aunt Iris's father.

Uncle Alf and Auntie Iris on the steps of St. Michael of all Angels

By the age of 14, I was a typical teenager and my school work began to lapse as I did not pay as much attention to my lessons as I should have. The only lesson I did enjoy and which I did not play up at was 'Housewifery' which basically was learning how to cook. We had to take our own ingredients and this lesson would be every other week. I thoroughly enjoyed that. On the weeks we didn't have Housewifery, we had Needlework which I absolutely loathed and was never very good at, much to the disappointment of my mum who as I mentioned previously was a very clever needlewoman. I would say to her "Mum I can't be good at everything". She would reply "Well Maureen what are you good at?" She would be even more scathing and say that my ability to sew was only fit for mail sacks. That was a bit below the belt because academically I wasn't bad at all.

In the summer of 1956 mum and dad booked a holiday for one week on Canvey Island. They had rented out a bungalow. We didn't have a car in those days so we went by bus and train. The train took us to Benfleet where we caught a bus to Canvey Sea Front; from there we walked down a side turning which led to the bungalow.

It was nicely situated and the bungalow itself was neat and tidy. It had 3 bedrooms, mum and dad in one, Veronica and I in another and Barry had the small room on his own.

That summer was particularly warm and sunny and we would spend most of our days on the sandy beach. Mum would pack sandwiches and as a treat we were given pocket money to buy ice-cream. For entertainment we would walk along the sea front to the Arcade where there were fruit machines and a small funfair, with rides and I liked the Helter Skelter which was fun. Holidays were few and far between as mum and dad didn't have much money and we would mostly go to Nanny Betts in

Chelveston and spend the 2 weeks in July that dad always booked for his summer holidays. We would of course have days out but I did enjoy the rare treat of a seaside holiday.

Soon I had to start thinking about what I wanted to do when I left school. As my Uncle Ted was a Chef and I enjoyed cooking so much, my first choice was to go into catering and train as a chef, but mum turned me off of that by saying that it was long hours, and not very much pay. Then I thought of my other love of flowers, couldn't I learn Floristry? Again my mum came up with reasons for not doing this. I was at a loss knowing what to do. Then she said "Why don't you go into an office and I will pay for you to go to evening classes to learn Shorthand and Typing". Not having any other options I agreed. So she enrolled me into evening classes at the Joseph Barratt School in Walthamstow. I had to attend on a Monday and Tuesday night. So in September 1956 I began classes.

I enjoyed doing the shorthand classes to begin with but it is a very difficult skill to learn and I soon fell behind. However my typing was coming on very well.

By this time as mentioned previously, I had met up with some boys that Marion knew and we started to hang around with them. One of them, whose name was Donald Stitchbury, starting paying a lot of attention to me. I agreed to walk out with him and asked mum if I could bring him home to tea. Donald was a very polite boy, who always dressed in a nice suit shirt and tie. Mum liked him. He would always bring a little gift for her, of either a box of chocolates or a bunch of flowers. We would still hang around in the crowd with the other lads. There was a Harry Baldwin whom I quite liked and had walked out with him for a short while, but then Marion had fancied him as well so he went with her. Then there was Roy Spooner, Dennis McKenzie and last but not least Roy Shanks.

After a little while I began to get a bit tired of Donald. He was very clingy and he never had a sense of humour and would never understand a joke. By this time, I had noticed Roy Shanks as he was the quietest of the bunch and I thought he was very good looking. He had the most beautiful blue eyes I have ever seen with long dark lashes. He wasn't very tall, and was quite slim. He was almost 17. So I started to flirt with him, which of course made Donald jealous. Strangely enough Donald and Roy both worked for a firm called Myra Shoe Works in Leyton and one day when they were at work, Donald had a word with Roy saying that I was his girlfriend and in so many words warned Roy to stay away from me, but Roy told Donald that we liked each other.

In the meantime, Donald's brother was getting married, and unknown to me Donald had approached my mum and asked if he could take me to the wedding. Of course mum readily agreed. So when Donald told me, I was furious and said that I didn't want to go. However, my mum did finally persuade me, by letting me wear make up for the first time. So Donald called for me on the day of the wedding, and we went to his house which was opposite to the one where Roy lived in Priors Croft. I should explain that Priors Croft was only a 5 minute walk from where I lived in the centre of Priory Court and to reach it I just had to walk to the end of the estate and turn left. The wedding took place in the local Church St. Andrews which was in Higham Hill Road. It was a bitterly cold day in October and like all churches, it was cold and draughty.

The reception was held at a restaurant in Walthamstow Market and we all sat down to a meal which was quite nice. After the meal was over, we sat around for a time, and then I suggested to Donald that we slip away and go to Priory Court where they were having a concert. He reluctantly agreed so I got my way.

As soon as we arrived at the Community Centre we found the others and sat with them, but I sat with Roy all night much to Donald's annoyance. When I look back now, it was a nasty thing to do.

On 5th November 1956, and a week before my 15th birthday - we had our usual bonfire on the allotments at the rear of L Block where we cooked potatoes on the fire and it was like a party with all the residents from the block joining in. Roy and the other boys came and also Marion and we had a good night. There was a huge bonfire on the allotment and the children from the block had spent weeks collecting all the wood and rubbish to pile onto the bonfire. They had made a guy which was then stuck on the top. At 6 o'clock one of the dads set the bonfire alight and it flared up and there was a big cheer from all the people gathered round. Then the fireworks started which was mainly set off by the dads, although there were other teenagers there who had their own fireworks and in particular one firework I hated was the Jumping Jack because when it was set off near a person no matter where they went it appeared to follow, and I had had that happen to me on a couple of occasions, so I stood well back and watched the proceedings away from the main crowd.

Roy and the others were standing with me when pulling me aside Roy asked me to go out with him, and I said yes. That was the end of the romance or not as the case may be; with Donald Stitchbury. I didn't see much of him after that as he no longer hung around with the others. Roy and I started going out together, although he still kept in touch with his friends, and for the first year he would choose them over me when it came to going fishing or shooting.

The following week was my birthday and Roy presented me with a net underskirt made of different layers of coloured stiffened net which all the girls wore beneath their flared skirts. I was so pleased with it, and thanked Roy so much. He confessed that he had been too shy to go into the shop and buy it so he had sent his mate Dennis in.

When I showed my mum she was horrified "I don't think that is very nice, a boy buying you underwear" she said. I told her to move on with the times. I am ashamed to admit that I was not very nice to my mum at this time in my life. My teenage hormones were raging and of course at the ages of 14 to 17 girls are usually finding their own personalities, but I always felt my mum wanted to control me, I now understand why and that she worried about me.

There was one particular incident where I had dropped some soiled clothes into the linen bin in the bathroom and mum had had something soaking in a bowl of bleach by the side of the bin. I had been a bit careless when throwing the clothes in and one of them had missed and dropped into the bowl of bleach. Mum found this and went absolutely mad at me. She had been on at me for some time now, "Clean you room" "Put your clothes away" and "You don't help me in the house, I'm working all day" - which was untrue since I had to stay in every Sunday dusting and polishing for her. She never seemed to have a go at my sister Veronica who was quite untidy but I was blamed for her mess. I just got fed up with her nagging, and this incident was the last straw. As she ranted and raved at me, I suddenly lost my temper and went for her with every intention of hitting her. Luckily my dad stepped in and managed to calm the situation. I did apologise afterwards, but still felt put upon. Whenever I think of it now I feel very ashamed of my actions. She worked very long hours and was not very well.

My mum did try to persuade me to go out with other boys but by the time I was 16 I knew that Roy was the one. I was still continuing my evening classes and would study with my friend Jacqueline who also lived in Priory Court.

In December 1956 my mum came with me for an interview at a local firm as a junior and I was offered the job at £2.10s (£2.50p) per week which I accepted. I was to commence my employment in January 1957.

So I was leaving school days behind and entering into the grown-up world of work.

Maureen in Epping Forest circa 1957

Roy with his mates Dennis and John in Priors Croft

Roy in Lloyds Park circa 1957

CHAPTER EIGHT

1957 – 1959 – First Holiday and engagement

In January 1957 I started my job in the offices of a Cable company which was situated quite locally in Sutherland Road. There were two other girls in the office, both of whom were older than me. Margaret Bird was about 18 and engaged to be married. She had been with the company for about 3 years. Then there was Jill who was the Managing Director's Secretary. My job was to do the filing make the tea and take correspondence into the Factory Manager's office. Another lady called Irene worked for the factory Manager. The hours were quite long. I started at 9 a.m. until 6 p.m. but on Mondays and Tuesday I was allowed to go half an hour earlier as I had my evening classes.

I got on quite well with Margaret and Jill and was often sent out on errands to the Post Office or out to get some shopping for them. I didn't really have much to do with the Director. I learned quite a bit whilst I was there and was allowed to practise my typing.

My romance with Roy was going well, and we would go to the cinema at weekends, that was when he wasn't going fishing of course. He belonged to the Walthamstow Avenue Fishing Club and went out with them every other Sunday during the fishing season which ran from 16 June to 15 March the following year.

Saturday afternoons in the summer Roy would come round for me and we would walk to Walthamstow Market and look at all the stalls and sometimes I would buy odds and ends. Then often when they were in season, we would buy a bag of cherries and eat them as we walked along the High Street. The market was very busy and crowded with people searching for bargains and the stallholders would be shouting their wares to entice people to buy from them I loved going to Walthamstow Market and enjoyed the atmosphere.

Near to the top half of the High Street was a cinema called the Carlton where Roy and I would often go on a Saturday night. We would sit in the back row and of course it was very dark inside the auditorium so we would amuse ourselves when other patrons came into the cinema and because it was so dark they were unable to see where they were going and instead of climbing the stairs to the row of seats, they would actually try to climb the seats themselves. Roy and I would be in fits of giggles, that is probably why we got on so well as we had the same sick sense of humour.

During the daytime there would be a stall outside the Carlton on which was sold a drink called Sarsaparilla. In the summer it was a cold drink and in the winter it would be a hot drink The stallholder would have an urn of hot water on the end of the stall; he would tip the Sarsaparilla into a small glass and then top it up with the hot water from an urn and would charge just 3d per glass. I would compare the taste to being something like liquorice; it was unique and very delicious. There were always lots of customers around the stall as it was very popular with many people. It was rumoured that the recipe for the drink was a family secret but sadly years later the stall was no longer there so I guess the family either didn't carry it on or they and it died out with them.

In the winter months the Chestnut man would stand outside the Carlton with a huge brazier full of hot coals on which he roasted Chestnuts at 6d (2½p) a bag and sold them to the people as they came out of the cinema. We would sometimes buy a bag of uncooked chestnuts and take them home and roast them ourselves. In those days most people had open fires. We would pull out the tray at the bottom of the fire into which the ash from the coals fell into, by attaching the fire tongs to the handle on the tray. We then placed chestnuts in the tray on top of the hot ash and then push it back under the fire after first cutting a cross in the top. The chestnuts would then come out blackened but cooked. We would use the fire tongs to pick them up very carefully so that we didn't burn ourselves and wait for them to cool off before eating them.

Roy and I would often go over Priory Court on a Thursday night to the Youth Club and on Saturday nights when they had put on a dance with a live band. Accompanying us would be Roy's brother Freddie who at 21 was 4 years Roy's senior and his girlfriend Barbara. Freddie and Barbara were engaged to be married and we all got along so well. Freddie and Roy were so alike when it came to having a sense of humour and Barbara and I would be in fits of giggles.

Freddie loved his football and was an Arsenal fan, much to the disgust of their eldest brother Jimmy who would rib him mercilessly as he was a Spurs fan. At that time Freddie was employed by Hitchmans Dairies as a Milk Rounds man. He played in a football league and was in a team representing Hitchmans Dairies. In 1956 his team won the league and Freddie and his team mates were presented with a small shield each to commemorate the occasion. (We still have this shield on our window sill to this day)

He had been a rather sickly child suffering from an enlarged heart muscle throughout his life and was in and out of hospital. Moll (their mum) always put it down to when Freddie had been evacuated during the war with his sisters Jean and Emmy. They had all been billeted with one family but for reasons known only to the people

138

concerned; they picked on Freddie and treated him badly. May be it was because he was a boy and they didn't liked boys, who knows?

Freddie had written home to his parents asking them to bring him back home but it wasn't his mum and dad who fetched him back but his brother Jimmy, who by this time was in the army. I have it on very good authority that those people did pay for what they did to Freddie, and not only did Jimmy bring him back home but his two sisters as well.

Meanwhile, there had been other bad news in the family. Roy's single sister June had discovered that she was pregnant and had tearfully told her parents. They immediately asked who the father was, but she said she didn't know – either that or she wasn't telling

Roy's other sister Jean had also got pregnant in 1954 and was engaged at the time and her fiancé was the father. She had had a girl and called her Teresa and had been allowed to bring the baby home. She had later married Bill Pope and went on to have another daughter Sharon with Bill.

This time around Roy's father Jim was adamant that when June had the baby she had to put it up for adoption. June went into labour in February 1957 and was taken into Thorpe Coombe Hospital where she gave birth to a baby girl whom she called Christine. Roy's other sisters all visited her and said how pretty the baby was. June cried when her elder sister Maisie visited and asked her to intervene and see if their father would relent and let June bring the baby home. Maisie suggested writing a letter so the next time she visited she gave June a pen and some writing paper and June wrote a heartfelt letter to her dad promising that she would work hard for the baby and that they would not be a burden on her parents.

It must have had the effect because Jim relented and June was allowed to bring Christine home leaving very unhappy couple who had been hoping to adopt Christine. True to her word June put Christine in the Nursery and was soon back to work. The child never wanted for anything and if the truth was known she was thoroughly spoilt by both Jim and Moll. In fact when they both retired they practically brought her up.

Meanwhile, Freddie was still enjoying his life and he never let this illness get in the way, so it was a bit of a shock when in April 1957 he became ill and had to be rushed to North Middlesex Hospital. Roy and I visited him with his mum and dad and Freddie really looked unwell, but he was the same old Freddie laughing and joking in spite of his illness.

On 10th May 1957 a policeman knocked on the door of number. 32 Priors croft where the family resided with the sad news that Freddie had passed away early that morning. Of course everyone was devastated not least Roy because he had been so close to his brother.

Moll found it hard to come to terms with the news because she and their dad, Jim Senior had visited Freddie the previous evening and as they left after visiting hours had finished they had looked back at the hospital to the room where Freddie was and he was up at the window waving to them. Moll was convinced that Freddie knew he wouldn't be seeing them again.

The funeral was arranged for the following week and I asked Margaret if I could have the day off. She spoke to the Director who said I could. So on the morning of the funeral I walked round to Roy's house, all the family were there, including Barbara and her family. As you might expect, the atmosphere was one of sadness and disbelief that such a young man who had everything to look forward to had passed away. I didn't go to the actual funeral but remained in the family home and helped Roy's Cousin Flossie and his Aunt to prepare the food for the wake. It seemed hours and hours before the family returned.

Freddie had been interred at Chingford Mount Cemetery. Jim senior had purchased a plot which was designed to take 3 coffins so when the time came he and Moll would join their son.

I tried to comfort Roy as much as I could but he just cried and I felt the tears falling as I held on to him.

Roy had another brother Frank who was a Sergeant in the regular Army and had managed to get compassionate leave. He had been conscripted into National Service and had enjoyed Army life so much that when the conscription came to an end he had joined up again. He had seen a lot of action and had been in Kenya fighting the Mau Mau and at one time had been reported missing in action which must have been awful for his parents. However he had been found unharmed although his best friend had been blown up as they tried to crawl underneath a wire fence. Their commanding office had been inexperienced and had led his men into enemy territory, but they had somehow found their way back to their own lines.

Frank was engaged to be married to a girl called Jacky who was 9 years younger than him and just a year older than me. She came from the Portsmouth area and she and I got on really well. She was a pretty girl with blonde hair and a couple of years previously she had been voted Carnival Queen of Portsmouth. Frank and Jacky obviously loved one another deeply and just got engaged, but no date had yet been set for their wedding.

The next day I returned to work and Margaret asked me if everything had gone off ok and I broke down in tears as I remembered the good times that Roy and I had had with Freddie and Barbara.

Margaret was engaged to be married and her fiancé's name was Roy Woollard. They had arranged their wedding for June of the following year. He was quite a nice chap and was about 5 years older than Margaret. One day she came in very excited and said that she and Roy had found a place of their own and would begin to furnish it ready to move into when they got married. Irene was also a very good friend of Margaret's and they were always gossiping with each other, and Jill sometimes joined in. At times I felt very much like the outsider as the three girls did not include me in their conversations.

Most Sunday's during the summer months Roy would call for me after I had finished the housework and we would get on a bus to The Rising Sun in Woodford New Road and stroll through Epping Forest, stopping at the lake watching the swans and ducks, and people would take rowing boats out onto the lake. We did that once but because of my fear of the water I was a bit scared that the boat would tip. There were other times that I would do the housework on a Saturday and then Roy and I would have a whole day together on a Sunday We would go to London on the train and see the sights, visiting the British Museum, Trafalgar Square and the Tower of London, which we both enjoyed so much.

In July of that year mum and dad had booked their annual holiday so I arranged to have the same time off from work. They had planned to visit my Nan and mum's other relations in Northamptonshire. Of course now I was seeing Roy I was a bit reluctant to go with them but mum insisted and said I could not stay on my own.

So I saw Roy on Friday night before we were due to go and said a tearful goodbye to him. Roy had also booked the same two weeks off and had planned to go out with his mates.

We arrived at Nan's house late Saturday afternoon. Nan had moved from Raunds and was now living on a small housing estate outside the village of Chelveston. Aunt Lil and her family lived next door. Mum and Dad shared a room with Veronica whilst Barry and I shared a room with Nan. She had put up a single bed for Barry and I was to sleep with Nan.

I missed Roy terribly and spent the first few days writing him letters. Mum had told Nan that I had a boyfriend and one day early in our first week, she asked me if I would like to invite him down to stay for the next week. I jumped at the idea and straight away I got out pen and paper and wrote a letter to him. Dad then wrote some directions down for him and I put those in with my letter. A couple of days later I got a reply from Roy saying yes he would be coming down that Saturday. So it was arranged that Uncle Walt would meet Roy at Rushden Bus Station and bring him back to Nan's house. I could hardly wait.

It was so nice to see Roy. I introduced him to my Nan and then we went next door to Auntie Lil where Roy would be sleeping. The boys Derek and Colin immediately took to him. Nan had made a big meal and we all sat down to eat.

During the week Roy and I went for long walks together and I showed him around the village of Chelveston. One day we went to Kettering Park which was a big open air park, which housed a zoo and picnic areas. Mum, dad Barry and Veronica came too It was a particularly lovely warm day, and after walking around for a while we decided to sit down at one of the many picnic tables provided. Mum had brought sandwiches and cakes in a wicker type bag, and some lemonade. Dad had spotted a small kiosk which sold tea and coffee so he went over and bought him and mum a cup of tea and we sat down and enjoyed the picnic and took photos. That day has remained in my memory as one of the nicest days I have spent.

Too soon the week was over and we all got ready to travel home. I thanked Nan for having us. Roy and I had bought Nan a little ornament in appreciation for putting us up and she was quite pleased with it. She took me to one side and said "I know that you are courting so don't you do anything that would disgrace the family". I said "Of course not Nan, I like Roy very much and we have been together for over 8 months now, he is my first serious boyfriend".

Towards the end of 1957 I had been with the company for a year and was getting a bit restless as I couldn't see any future in this job, so I decided to move on in order to improve my prospects and also to be able to utilise my typing skills much more. I scanned the jobs vacancy page in the local Guardian Newspaper and saw a job advertised for a junior typist in a company called Caribonum. They were large manufacturers in Leyton producing carbon paper and other office requisites. I phoned up and was offered an interview for the following week. I went along feeling very nervous, this was only my second job and my mum and had been with me for my first interview. However the Personnel lady was very pleasant and made me feel at ease. After a short discussion when she had explained what the job entailed and all about holidays, sick pay and wages, I was offered the job. I told her that I had to give one weeks' notice. She said she would write and confirm my appointment that day and it was arranged that I would start after Christmas.

I went back to work after my interview, and asked to see the Director, and was shaking as I entered his office. I tendered my resignation and explained the reason why I was leaving. He accepted and said he was sorry to see me go as he thought I had come along in leaps and bounds since I had started with the company. I thanked him, went back into the General Office where Margaret and Jill were busy working. I hadn't said anything to either of them and Margaret was obviously curious as to why I had seen the Director. So I told the two girls that I would be leaving at Christmas which was a week away. Margaret was surprised at this and asked me why, so I told her that I didn't see there was any future if I stayed as obviously both Margaret and Jill had good jobs there and I couldn't see either of them leaving any time soon. Margaret said she understood and both she and Jill wished me well and asked all about the new job I would be taking up in the New Year.

Feeling very nervous I caught the bus to Leyton to start my new the job January 1958. I was introduced to the people I would be working with. The office was much larger than I had been used to working in and I soon got to know the people there. The job was explained to me which was pretty simple. The first day went very quickly and I felt a bit better at the end that at least I had got that over with.

I wanted very much to improve on my typing, and apart from work, the only other opportunity I had to do any long pieces of typing was at evening classes. I was discussing this with Roy one day when he surprised me by offering to buy me a typewriter so that I could practise. So that weekend we visited a local typewriter shop and he bought me a lovely Olympia Portable typewriter in light grey which came in its own metal case. It was quite heavy to carry but I loved it, and I still have the typewriter to this day, although it is never used anymore.

To begin with the job wasn't too bad; it involved typing up orders on yellow slips. I did make a few mistakes as my typing wasn't all that good at that time, but nevertheless I quite enjoyed it and made some friends there. Part of my duties was to go into the factory and take these slips to the relevant offices. There were a few boys working in the factory and I got a few wolf whistles, and I went very red with embarrassment.

After 3 months at the company I was called into the Manager's office one day and he told me that my work was not up to scratch therefore he had no alternative but to terminate my employment and I was to go that day with a week's money in lieu of notice. I was absolutely devastated and felt such a failure. I came out of his office in tears, and because I was so embarrassed I went straight to the Ladies toilets and cried my eyes out. One of the older ladies I had worked with came into the toilet and saw me crying and asked me what was wrong. I told her what had happened. She put her arms around me and "Don't worry love, I am sure you will get another job quite easily, don't let this put you off, just keep practising your typing – I know how you feel because I was sacked from my first job but it might be a good thing, as something better will come along". I did feel a bit better after that but I was so ashamed that I had been sacked.

I got home that night and dreaded having to tell mum and dad, but they were ok about it and I did have a week's money to fall back on until I got another job.

I began my search for work the following Monday and first of all I approached an Agency to see if they had any available positions, luckily they did have one vacancy on their books for a copy typist working for the London Rubber Company situated in Hall Lane Chingford. The lady at the Agency phoned through to the company and arranged for me to go for an interview that day. She very kindly gave me directions how to get there and what bus route to take

I arrived at the company on time and was shown into the Manager's office and he introduced himself as Mr.Ross-Turner. I was not quite as nervous as I had been at my previous interview and relaxed a bit more and answered all his questions. At the end of the interview Mr.Ross-Turner offered me the job and told me I could start the next day. I had been asked why I had left my other job, I admit that I did tell a little white lie and said that there were no prospects so I had decided to leave. I told them that I was going to evening classes to learn shorthand and typing and Mr.Ross-Turner was quite impressed by this.

So I settled in to my third job in March 1958 and I really did enjoy working there. I was taught how to use the duplicator and how to type stencils. In fact the company sent me for a day's training in London to learn the intricacies of using the Roneo Duplicator.

I made friends with the other older ladies who worked in the office and a couple of girls around my age, one of whom was called Pauline and she and I became really good friends.

My former colleague Margaret married her fiancé on 15th June 1958 I hadn't been invited to the wedding, although I believe both Irene and Jill together with their respective partners did go, but I did go along to the church to see their wedding.

My Roy in the meantime had also changed jobs and left the shoe company and got a job working at the Tip Top Dyers and Cleaners where both our mothers worked, together with two of his sisters. I used to see him on Wednesday, Thursday and Friday nights and sometimes on a Saturday if he wasn't going fishing the next day. We would go for long walks together and particularly liked to go to Lloyds Park where I took a lot of photographs with my little Box Brownie camera which my Auntie Jinnie had left to me.

As both of our mums played darts we would also go to the Darts Presentation Dances which were held at the Assembly Hall in Walthamstow. This was and still is a lovely building which is situated by the Walthamstow Town Hall. I believe that both buildings were constructed in the 1930's. The Town hall lies back from the road in its own grounds, in front of which is a pond and in the centre of the pond there is a large fountain. The Town hall is reached through big iron gates off of Forest Road which leads down a driveway and then it winds round to the front of the Town Hall building itself. It is an imposing white building with rows of steps leading to the entrance. There is a clock tower on the top of the main building. The grounds are always well kept with colourful flower beds of whatever plants happen to be in season. Every one admires the building as it is quite famous and a focal point in Walthamstow. The Assembly Hall is built of the same construction and bricks as the Town hall which blends in so well. This building is on the right of the Town Hall and also has steps going up to the entrance.

Walthamstow Town hall and Assembly Hall.

As time went on I used to miss Roy so much when he went fishing that he invited me to go along. Roy and his friends would go on a coach on a Sunday morning, so it meant I had to be up early. They used different fishing venues and I would take along a book to read. As I was the only girl on the coach I earned the name *'Duchess'* and they made a great fuss of me. I did find the fishing very boring and could not see the point in sitting on a bank just staring at the water and the float bobbing up and down hoping that some poor fish would come along and take the bait. But at least I got to spend the day with Roy, even though he had his eye on his float most of the time, and I was not allowed to make a noise in case I scared the fish way. It was nicer in the summer as Roy would take a blanket and lay it out on the grass, so I would take a book and sometimes some knitting to occupy my time whilst Roy fished. However winter was a different kettle of fish (forgive the pun) and I would sometimes decline to accompany him.

I also went out with Roy and his friends John and Dennis and one day was horrified when he caught an eel and holding it in an old piece of towel he laid the eel's head on a post and bashed it until it was dead. Oh I thought that was so cruel. He wrapped the eel up and took it home and gave it to my mum who left it to soak in a bowl of salted water. She would then later boil it up and leave it so that the juices went to jelly. My brother being curious went to touch the eel and it moved, because the nerves stay live in eels for a long time. He nearly jumped out of his skin, and we all burst out laughing. In spite of this I do like jellied eels, not to everyone's taste I must admit, but they are nice, if you don't think how they were caught and killed.

As time went on Roy and I became more serious about each other. We didn't have a lot of money so we would visit our relations. Thursday nights we would visit his sister Maisie and her husband Bert and their daughter Colleen.

Some Sunday nights we would go to the pictures and then get on a bus and visit his sister Jean and her husband Bill and their two daughters Teresa and Sharon.

My mum and dad had accepted that Roy and I were together but there were still rules. I had to be in by 10.30 during the week and 11 o'clock on Friday and Saturdays. I did obey those rules most of the time.

Sometimes on a Sunday Roy and I would to go to the cinema. I much preferred the Granada cinema to all the others as it was quite grand inside. There was a cinema attendant who had been working at the Granada for many years whose name was Ernie. He was the one who used to chuck us out if we tried to sneak in without paying when we were younger. Of course I shouldn't think he recognised either me or Roy.

The kiosks was on the left as you entered and we would buy our tickets, and then proceed through the big double doors into a larger foyer in the middle of which was the sweet counter. Roy would treat me to a box of Poppets, or we would have a quarter of Bassets Allsorts, and a quarter of toffees. Roy would buy the best tickets which cost 3s.9d which were for the seats upstairs. So after purchasing our sweets we would go up the big winding staircase into the darkened cinema where we were shown to our seats by the Usherette. We usually chose the back row where we would get a good view of the screen. At half time, Roy would buy ice-creams and a drink. Roy smoked in those days, but would roll his own so he would get himself an ounce of Golden Virginia Tobacco. He had a little machine on which he would place the cigarette paper then he would take a pinch of tobacco from his tin and roll it into a sausage shape, place it in the machine and turn the rollers and it would roll the paper around the tobacco, then he would take the rolled cigarette out lick the sticky part of the cigarette paper and stick in down. In time he dispensed with the machine and just rolled his own.

One Sunday there was a film at the Granada that we both wanted to see, and Roy's sister Jean had invited us round to tea after the film. I told mum and dad where I was going. I remember it was around November time and when we arrived at the cinema late afternoon, it was getting dark and there was a mist was forming.

We enjoyed the film and came out a couple of hours later by which time the mist had turned to fog and was getting quite thick. We had no means of getting in touch with Jean to cancel our visit so we decided to carry on.

Jean lived with her husband Bill and two daughters, Teresa and baby Sharon, in Chelmsford Road Walthamstow. We had to get a bus along Hoe Street and got off about 5 stops along. From there we crossed the road and walked the rest of the way.

Jean made us both a nice cup of tea as we were quite cold by this time. We had a lovely meal and stayed about 2 -3 hours. Roy looked out of her window and said that the fog was quite thick so we had better make a move home.

We left Jean's around 9 o'clock and walked down to Hoe Street to catch a bus. We waited and waited but no buses came along so we decided to walk. I had bought some new shoes which I had worn for the first time that day, and they began to rub the backs of my heels. It took a good two hours to walk all the way home to Priory Court, so by the time we arrived it was about 11 o clock. My dad was waiting on the door step as we got out of the lift and he was furious and wanted to know where I had been. I tried to explain to him about the fog and the lack of buses but he just would not listen and told me to get inside. I said a quick goodnight to Roy and went in. I felt so embarrassed that he had shown me up in front of Roy.

When I took my shoes off my heels were red raw with blisters. By this time my dad had calmed down and I was able to explain to him the reason why I was so late. I asked him if he had looked out of the window and seen how thick the fog was. He said that was why he had been so worried. I told him that I understood but I was with Roy and nothing would have happened to me. I showed him the blisters and he realised that I had been telling the truth. Looking back now, I fully understand how worried my parents must have been, we didn't have a phone in those days so there was no way I could have got in touch to warn them I would be late, but at the time, I was angry that he had not trusted me or Roy and listened to me in the first place.

Roy had become tired of working at the Tip Top Cleaners and his brother Jimmy had offered him the opportunity of working with him erecting Pylons. The only downside was that it was often away from home, but it was good money, a lot more than he had been earning at the Cleaners. Roy and I discussed this and we both agreed that the sacrifice would be worth it so that we could save up to get married.

We were both serious about each other and wanted to spend our lives together so plucking up courage Roy asked my dad if we could get engaged on my 18th birthday that November and dad agreed. He even said that he would hire the Community Centre for a party for us.

So in January 1959 Roy started work with Jimmy and their first job was in Crowborough in Suffolk, which wasn't too bad as they were able to get home each night. This job lasted about 4 weeks. It was January and very cold and it had begun to snow and it wasn't an easy job building the pylons. Roy's job was to climb up the mast and fix the wires going across between the pylons.

The next job that came up was in Dover. Again it was cold and icy weather and they had some snow. The pylons were erected on the famous White Cliffs of Dover and each time we have travelled to Dover he has pointed these out and said "I helped to build those pylons".

That job ended and the next one was in South Wales. This was different obviously because of the distance involved, they had to find lodgings. Jimmy had told him that they would be away for four weeks at a time, then would come home on a Friday and return on the Monday. It was very lonely without him and I missed him so much, but we did have our letters. I was a very prolific letter writer whereas Roy on the other hand, used to space his words out so much that it looked as if he had written a lot to me, when in fact he could probably have fitted it all on one or two sheets of paper.

At that time we didn't have a telephone so Roy and I devised a system whereby he would arrange to ring me on the telephone box down the road at 8 o clock on a Thursday night. I remember this because that was the night we would watch 'Rawhide' on the television. I would be anxious that no-one would be using the telephone box at the allotted time and most of the time it was empty. It was so nice to hear his voice, and I always felt tearful when we had to ring off.

Meanwhile my job was going well and I was given more responsibility helping out the old gentleman who had worked in the Advertising Department for many years. His name was Aubrey he was nearing retirement and must have been in his late sixties, obviously passed retirement age. He was of short stature and walked with a stoop. He wore glasses and very rarely smiled thus gaining a reputation for being surly. He was always smartly dressed with a dark suit, an immaculate white shirt and a dark tie. A lot of people didn't get along with him finding him to be rather abrupt, but I liked him and he liked me and so he allowed me to help him. We would chat about all kinds of things and he would tell me about his past life and his beloved wife. They had no children but he did have a little Corgi called Megan, whose photo was pinned up in the stationery cupboard. That put me on a good footing with him because of course, I loved dogs.

He was responsible for handing out stationery to the staff who worked in the various departments and he had to record the stock levels and re-order when they were getting low, so he taught me how to do this.

There were four other women in the Advertising department who were senior to me and with whom I had a good relationship with. Pauline and I were still quite good friends, she and her boyfriend Tom had become engaged to be married but had not set a date. We would go out in a foursome sometimes to the cinema and on one occasion we enjoyed a day out in Southend-on-Sea.

One day a new girl joined the company in the Advertising Department. At first it was nice to have someone around my own age. Her name was Christine, and we got talking and to my surprise I found out that she had got married at the age of 17. She told Pauline and I that her husband was in the army had been posted away from home so they had decided to get married. Pauline soon became very good friends with Christine, and in due course, she dropped me and I was left out of their conversations.

Pauline then announced that she and Tom had set the date for their wedding for July 1960 and I congratulated her and hoped that she had a lovely day. I found out that Christine was loaning Pauline her wedding dress, veil and headdress as Pauline and Tom didn't have a lot of money. Pauline had recently been reunited with her father who was divorced from her mother, and had been estranged from Pauline for some years. I think it was this that had made her decide to bring her wedding forward. Her father had found them a small flat to rent and Pauline said that she would ask her dad to give her away. Pauline Christine and I would sit together in the canteen at lunchtimes, but more often than not they would be in conversation with each other and I would feel ostracised by them. Eventually I stopped going to the canteen with them, although I still remained friends with both of them.

Aubrey finally retired after a few months and our Manager asked me to take over the job that he had done which was counting the advertising slips that came in and putting them into their respective boxes, and sending out free samples of contraceptives. I also took over the stationery issuing and re-ordering the stock.

I should explain that the London Rubber Company were producers of rubber products including the famous brand of contraceptives Durex.

Another lady called Audrey joined the company soon after Aubrey had retired. We got talking she was in her late 20s and married and had initially trained as a nurse, but had decided to give it up to go back to office work Before taking up nursing she had been a shorthand-typist earning quite good money, and that was the reason she had decided to return to this vocation. She soon initiated herself into the department and before long she was picked to carry out various tasks for our Manager. I was a bit envious of this since I thought that this had been my opportunity to get on. I was still studying shorthand and typing, although the shorthand was by now a bit half-hearted as I had concentrated more on my typing. This had improved by quite a bit and I was up getting a good speed.

During all this time of course, Roy was away and mum started to try to encourage me to go out with other boys. She tried to drip poison into my ear by saying "Do you think that Roy is sitting alone each night – no – he is probably chatting up all the Welsh girls and having a good time, while you – you silly cow – stay at home moping each night waiting for him to call you on Thursday nights and to come home after a month" This did upset me a bit and a part of me did wonder if Roy fancied any Welsh girls. He did tell me once when he came home that he and Jimmy and his other workmates would visit this café each night for their meal and a particular waitress would rush up to serve them. I think she really liked Roy, and Roy played on it. Basically he was a good man very loyal and faithful and I did trust him.

On one of his weekends home we decided to go to Walthamstow High Street, I had a few bits and pieces to buy and we wandered along looking in all the shops. We came to Fish Brothers which was a well-known jewellers and Roy suddenly announced that he wanted to buy me a necklace. We looked in the window and then he suggested that we go inside. Roy pushed the shop door open and a bell rang inside then a shop assistant came forward "Good afternoon, can I help you?" she said. Roy said we were just browsing, and then looking at the display beneath the counter I spotted an unusual bracelet. It had two thin gold chains and holding them together were gold letters spelling out the words 'My Darling'. I pointed it out to Roy and said how lovely it was and he asked me if I would like it. I said yes and we asked the shop assistant to show it to us.

I tried the bracelet on and although it was a bit loose it looked lovely. "I'll have it please" Roy said.

I wore it every day after Roy returned to Wales and everyone admired it. However one day I had popped across to the shops and bought some fruit and other bits and pieces. When I got back to the office, I looked down but my bracelet was missing. My heart skipped a beat. I immediately left the office and ran over to the last shop where I had done my shopping. "Excuse me; have you by any chance found a gold bracelet with the words 'My Darling' spelt out on it?" The man in the shop came forward and he had my bracelet in his hand. "Is this the one?" he asked. "Oh thank you so much I thought I had lost it". The man explained that he had found it on the floor after I had left and assumed that it belonged to me. That weekend I took the bracelet to the Jewellers and had a safety catch put on it.

Roy was due home again in June and he had suggested in one of his letters of buying me a, friendship ring. I thought that was a nice gesture but said why not buy an engagement ring instead? Even though we were officially getting engaged in November on my 18th birthday I could see no reason why we shouldn't get the rings now. So he agreed, but he said he would write to my dad first and ask him. However my dad wrote back and said no, saying we had already booked the Community Centre for November so we had to wait until then.

That weekend I went to the Market looking in all the Jewellers and spotted a lovely engagement ring which was 3 diamonds set into heart shapes on a twist. In hindsight perhaps I should have put a small deposit on the ring to secure it but I thought that it would still be there when Roy came home.

Much to my shame, I again I went against my dad's wishes. Roy came home for the weekend and on the 20th June 1959 Roy and I went to Fish Bros Jewellers in Walthamstow Market where I had seen the heart shaped

3 stone twist. To my disappointment it had been sold, so I looked at some other rings and finally chose another 3-stone Victorian twist engagement ring. I bought Roy an unredeemed thick gold buckle ring which had taken his fancy. The next step was to face my parents. My dad was absolutely furious, and looking back now, I can't say I blamed him. He told me in no uncertain terms that he would not allow me to get married until I was 21 – I was 17½ years old at that time. I said to Dad that we could still have our party as originally planned the only exception was that I already had the ring so it would be one less expense for the party. After he calmed down he agreed.

That evening we went out with Pauline and her fiancé Tom to celebrate. I was still friends with her, in spite of her actions towards me during work time. We spent the evening in a pub and had a good time.

In the meantime Roy was earning really good money and was sending it home and I was putting it into a joint Post Office Savings account together with money I saved from my wages.

On the 1st of July 1959 my new Cousin Michael was born to Auntie Iris and Uncle Alf so there was some cause for celebration and we were all invited to the Conservative club to wet the baby's head. At least it got me out for a while and I did enjoy myself.

During one of our visits to Maisie and Bert they suggested that we might like to go on holiday to the Isle of Wight with them in July. I was delighted to be invited but said I would have to ask my mum and dad. When I approached them their first reaction was 'no', but then when I told Maisie she said she would go and speak with them with the result that she persuaded them to let me go on holiday with them with the proviso that I behaved myself (whatever that meant!). So Maisie and Bert booked up rooms in the Boarding house and Roy was lodged in the house around the corner.

Roy came home from Wales a few days before we were due to go on holiday. It had been a particularly hot summer that year and when he came over to our flat he was suntanned and the sun had bleached his hair blond which he had had cut into a crew cut.

As he was now earning good money Roy had decided to have a suit made so he had taken himself off to John Colliers which was a local men's tailors and outfitters and had been measured up for the suit. He had chosen a light blue material for the suit. This was the first time I had seen him in his new suit and he did look extremely smart and the blue of the suit brought out the blue in his eyes coupled with a suntan he looked very handsome. He told me that when he had been on his way home he had been waiting for his train to come in and a couple of girls had approached him and asked if he was an American. Of course he played along and said yes in a false American accent.

At the end of July 1959 Roy and I met up with Maisie, Bert and Colleen and carrying our suitcases we all boarded a bus to take us to Tottenham Hale railway station where we would get a train to Waterloo and from there on to Portsmouth. From Portsmouth we would board a passenger ferry to take us across to the Isle of Wight and then on another train at Ryde to Sandown station.

My upset with Pauline was soon forgotten and I was determined to enjoy myself. It was a really lovely holiday, as it was the first time I had ever been to the Isle of Wight and instantly fell in love with it. We stayed in a boarding house in Carter Street which was run by a lady called Mrs. Grey. The house, in which we stayed, was a large house with quite a few bedrooms. It was very clean and spacious and the landlady Mrs. Grey looked after us well. Maisie and Bert had stayed with her previously so they all knew each other. Bert had booked the accommodation on a bed, breakfast and evening meal basis. It was a very popular Boarding House and the rooms were all occupied so Mrs. Grey had managed to get a room for Roy in her friend's boarding house around the corner, but he would come into our boarding house for his meals.

Other members of Roy's family also took their holiday in the same two weeks as us so we would all meet up on the beach. His mum had come along with his sister Alice her husband John and sons John Junior (or as he was affectionately known as 'little' Johnny) and Lenny. Also there was his sister June and her daughter Christine (who would later be one of my bridesmaids) his sister Emmy with her husband Ronny and two sons Malcolm and Terry, his sister Dolly, husband Joe and son Brian and last but not least Roy's younger brother David.

The weather was beautifully warm and sunny. We would spend each day on the beach where all the family had hired beach huts along the front at Sandown and had practically taken over, but everyone knew each other so it was very convivial and friendly. There was a little hut at the end which housed a camping stove and a kettle where we could go and make a cup of tea. Then we would go to the high street in Sandown to a shop which did lovely lunches and buy special rolls already made up with salad and ham.

Of an evening after dinner, we would meet up with other members of the family and go for a stroll along the cliffs, or sometimes we took the bus which travelled all over the island. My favourite pastime was walking along the beach once the tide had gone out and more often or not we would find money that people had dropped. We would clamber over the rocks and look in the rock pools for crabs. Because most of Roy's family were there it added to the fun. The tide would go out during the daytime quite a long way leaving a wide stretch of beach on which the whole family including the grandchildren would play rounder's or cricket. The best part was that I had Roy to myself for the whole 2 weeks. That was one of the best holidays I have ever had, and since that time the Isle of Wight has held wonderful memories for Roy and me.

One evening we all decided to take a bus to see Black gang Chine. In those days there was not that much erosion and there were lots of wooden steps going down the cliffs with rope bannisters to hold on to. The steps were lit up with fairy lights all the way down the cliff, it was quite precarious and I was a bit nervous walking down these little steps. However we soon reached the Chine itself and it was magical. There were lots of things to see and do and we spent a lovely evening there. Then of course, we had to go up the rickety steps again which quite hair-raising.

We also visited St.Catherines Lighthouse and Buddle Inn, Alum Bay where we were able to climb up the rocks and gather the coloured sand and put it into little glass containers. Over the years the cliffs became eroded and it was considered dangerous for people to climb them, so it is now forbidden. We visited Shanklin which is very quaint with lots of small shops and cafes. We had a drink in the Crab Inn, an old pub which is all lit up at night and has a pond in the front with lots of goldfish in it.

We also visited the Shanklin Chine and walked the whole length there and back. It was harder coming back since it was on a steep incline. The whole island was wonderful and appeared to be stuck in a time warp. Life was at a slower pace than back home in London. That is one of the reasons that it is so popular and why anybody who has had a holiday on the Isle of Wight feels really rested at the end of their holiday.

One day we were strolling along Sandown High Street looking in all the shops, and we stopped at one particular clothes shop where I saw a lovely housecoat. It was white with a small rose pattern printed on it. It had frilled Peter Pan collar and buttons down the front. I thought it would be ideal for my bottom drawer and commented on this, to my surprise Roy offered to buy it for me. I refused at first saying I would see how much money I had over at the end of the holiday and if I had enough, I would buy it for myself, but Roy insisted. So we went into the shop and fortunately they had one in my size. I was so pleased with it. I noticed that Maisie didn't say a word when I came out with the purchase, but I found out later that she had rather spitefully related this incident to Roy's mum saying that I was only with Roy for what he could buy me. I was rather upset at this because I had previously got on alright with her and it did put an edge on our relationship after that comment, so much so that we didn't visit her and Bert as often as we had before. I was rather a naïve teenager at that time and found it hard to stand up for myself. That of course changed over the years. However I did not let that spoil the memories of that lovely 2 weeks away.

I remained friends with Brenda, Jean, Marion and Georgina but we did not see very much of each other as of course we were all working and had other interests including boyfriends. I bumped into Marion's dad Jack one day in late 1959 and commented that I hadn't seen Marion recently. To my surprise he said that the whole family had moved to Canvey Island. Then he imparted a bit more news that shocked me when he told me that Marion was getting married and that she was expecting a baby. I asked him for their address on Canvey and I sat down and wrote to Marion. She replied soon after and said that she had got pregnant and her mum and dad had insisted that she get married and that her baby was due around the end of May, or beginning of June the next year. She said that her Nan had offered her a couple of rooms in the back of the shop where her grandparents lived and she was going to move in once she had the baby.

We continued to correspond as I didn't want to lose contact with her again. I saw quite a bit of Brenda and Jean as they lived in the same block. Brenda was in a serious relationship at the time.

Barry was now 15 years old and thinking of what career he wanted to pursue. He was very good with his hands and with making things. My mum's brother Bill had done photography as a hobby and was very good at it. He had been commissioned to take wedding photos and portraits for several of his friends, but had decided to give it up, so he had given all his equipment to Barry, who was a particular favourite of Uncle Bill. Barry had experimented and had managed to develop some photos but he never really took this interest further.

Barry decided that he would like to become an Engineer but first he would have to find a company which would employ him as an apprentice. He found such a company called Hammond and Champness. They were a local company based in Blackhorse Lane and manufactured lifts and components. Barry left school in July 1959 and in September started his new job as an apprentice Electrical Engineer. He was enrolled in college on a day-release programme, which he thoroughly enjoyed and learned his trade very quickly.

Veronica was now 10 years old and because she had contracted measles as a small child it had affected her eyesight so she had been prescribed with National Health glasses coupled with her straight hair and a fringe she looked like a character in one of the comics called 'Keyhole Kate' and that is what Roy had nicknamed her. Whenever mum and dad had gone over Priory Court Community Centre on a Friday to play Bingo and Roy happened to be home from Wales we spent the night watching TV. In order to get a bit of privacy we had bribed Barry and Veronica with some money to go out and get some sweets, but the little devils often sneaked back in and looked at us through the serving hatch having a little cuddle.

Finally November arrived and we were busy getting ready for our engagement party. Roy and I had gone out during the previous week and purchased food for the buffet in the evening. Mum and dad had paid for our engagement cake. All mum's family from Northampton were coming to the party as of course I was the first grandchild to get engaged. Roy and I had ordered two big bouquets for our respective mums. Regrettably Roy's family did not arrive with all the other guests. At that time Roy's dad Jim was a keen grower of Chrysanthemums which he would put into various shows and quite often won lots of prizes. The night of our engagement unfortunately clashed with one of his shows so all his family had gone to the show first. I was a bit upset over this but it couldn't be helped.

The weekend before our party I had gone to Walthamstow Market where there was a very nice shop called Davis's. After looking around I finally found a lovely white dress with black velvet flocked flowers all over the bodice and skirt. It had a 'V' neck with a fitted waist and a narrow belt to finish it off. The edge of the dress was scalloped with the black velvet. I bought it and put in in the wardrobe ready for our party the following week.

Of course everyone wanted to see my engagement ring which I had proudly worn for the previous four months. My mum's comment when I had first shown her my ring was "you should have chosen one with a good stone in it; you never know when you might need to pawn it as I have done with my engagement ring many times". My reply to that was "it is not how big the stones are mum but what it means and I hope I will never ever have to pawn it like you had to". I didn't want a solitaire like everyone else I wanted to be different.

The evening went really well, we had hired a band which we had used on previous family occasions, Discos were not heard of in those days. There were four people in the band; the compere was the lady who actually ran it and the band itself consisted of three men one on piano, one on drums and the other on the saxophone. Roy's family finally turned up about an hour and half later, although I was disappointed to note that none of them had made an effort to dress up for the occasion. During the interval Roy and I presented both our mums with a bouquet of flowers. All in all the evening went very well, and it was made all the more special because my Nan and my aunts and uncles had made the effort to come all the way from Northampton. The evening soon came to an end and everybody said how nice it had been.

In the meantime, Roy's parents had received a letter from his Brother Frank telling them that he was getting married on the 12th December 1959 in Portsmouth where his fiancée Jacky lived. So Jim Snr and Moll told the family and there were some discussions as to how we were all going to get there. One of Roy's brother-in-law's came up with an idea of hiring a coach. Everyone thought that would be a good idea so he offered to organise it and we would all chip in to pay for it.

On the day in question the coach arrived outside 32 Priors Croft. All the family had met up there as it was thought to be a good meeting point. We all clambered aboard the coach and we were soon on our way. It was a very cold day with the threat of snow, not the kind of day for a wedding. Frank had stayed at his parents' house overnight and was on the coach with us having come home on leave a few days previously. It was then he surprised Roy by asking him to be his Best Man. At that time Roy was quite shy and he was so taken aback that he declined so their elder brother Jimmy stepped in. Frank directed the coach driver to Jacky's parents' house which was a cottage off the main road into Portsmouth. We went in for a celebratory drink before continuing on to the village of Southwark, Hampshire where the wedding would be taking place in the village church.

The Church was quite old and sat back off the main road than ran through the village. The coach parked up and we all walked into the church. It was so beautiful inside; it had been decorated with flowers tied to the end of each pew. On either side of the Alter were huge flower displays of white carnations and fern in tall vases.

Frank and Jimmy sat in the front pew and not long afterwards the bride arrived with her bridesmaids. We were all asked to stand and Jacky walked down the aisle on the arm of her father. She wore a ballerina length wedding gown in white lace with a short veil which was attached to a circlet of flowers. She carried a small bouquet of white carnations and fern.

When the ceremony was over, we went outside for the photos to be taken. It was freezing cold and I was shivering. We then got back on the coach – Frank had given the driver directions to the hall where the reception was held.

Frank and Jacky left after the reception to go on honeymoon whilst the rest of us enjoyed the party. Around 11 o' clock we got on to the coach for the journey home. We were all in a jolly mood and one of Roy's brother-in-laws's said to Roy "Well you're next Roy". Roy replied "I don't think so, not yet anyway". I was quite upset at this remark considering that we had just become engaged a few months ago, and had only celebrated our engagement the month before. I remonstrated with him and he said "I didn't mean it to come out that way; I just meant that we wouldn't be getting married just yet until we have saved a bit more".

Roy went back to Wales after the wedding, but it would only be for a couple of weeks and then it would be Christmas. Roy had intimated before he went back that he was homesick and hated being away, but said the money was good and we needed it so that we could save for our wedding.

*Maureen and Roy at the Darts Presentation Dance
At Walthamstow Assembly Hall.*

Roy and Jimmy returned home just before Christmas and as a special treat, I was allowed to go to the Christmas party at Roy's parents' house but I had to be home by 12 so Roy made sure that we complied with my parents' wishes and we left his house at quarter to 12 arriving home on time. We said goodnight to each other and I went indoors. Mum was waiting up for me and asked if I had had a good time, and I said yes I had.

There was a New Year's Eve party over the Community Centre and I asked Roy if he would like to go and he said yes it would make a change. Mum and Dad Barry and Veronica also attended. They had hired a band and many people turned up from the flats, most of whom we knew from other events. So when midnight arrived we all welcomed in the New Year and each and every one of us wondered what 1960 would bring.

Maureen and Roy at Freddie's grave 1957
Margaret and Roy's wedding day 15 June 1958

Roy, Colleen, Bert and Maisie in their garden at Palmerston Road Walthamstow.

Tom and Pauline at Southend-on-Sea

Roy and Maureen on Ryde Pier Isle of Wight July 1959

Bert, Maisie, Colleen, Maureen and Roy on Sandown Beach, Isle of Wight.

Roy & Maureen with Jim & Moll, Nanny Penn, and Mum and Dad at their engagement November 1959

Roy and Maureen's engagement photograph

CHAPTER NINE

1960 – 1961 – Planning our wedding

One Thursday soon after Roy had returned to Wales I waited in the phone box as usual. I had not received any letters from Roy for over a week and began to worry. The phone rang and I picked up the receiver and Roy's voice was at the other end. "Why haven't you been writing lately" I asked, he paused then said something that sent chills down my spine, "I have had an accident, I fell down the pylon about 30 feet or so and sprained my ankle and burnt all of my hands" I was distraught and asked him what had happened, and he explained that he was fixing the spacer on the line and had told the man below to swing it over but Roy had not caught it and lost his footing and had fallen down the pylon. Luckily he had managed to grab the rope as he fell and this had caused 'rope burn' resulting in him having to have his hands bandaged up. That was the reason he had been unable to write to me. He had hit the ground with such a thump that Jimmy had run over fearing the worse that Roy was dead. It must have been an awful shock for him. Luckily Roy had only been knocked out. He said he was ok, but I think that was the turning point, because a couple of months later he told Jimmy that he wanted to quit and was leaving.

Ironically a few months after Roy's accident one of his best friends also fell off the pylon but he was not so lucky and was killed instantly.

I worried myself sick after that. Then one day, as I was coming out of work, Roy was standing there. I was surprised to see him as it wasn't his weekend to come home. That was when he told me that he had quit, he had got so fed up with the job and he said that his brother Jimmy had been especially hard on him all the time. I suspect that Jimmy did that so that the other men couldn't accuse him of favouritism. So Roy now had to look for another job. At that time his dad worked for Bowater Scott's who manufactured paper products including toilet and kitchen rolls in their factory situated in St. Andrews Road in Walthamstow. So Roy's dad spoke to the Foreman to see if there were any vacancies and he was told to send Roy for an interview.

Roy went along the next day and was offered the job. The only downside was that it was shift work. There were three shifts, 6 a.m. to 2 p.m., 2 pm to 10 p.m. 10 p.m. to 6 a.m. on a weekly basis. Roy took the job anyway. It wasn't as much money as he had been earning but at least he would be safe.

For the next 10 months he worked at Bowater's. It was hard getting used to the different working hours but he managed it, and when he was on the early shift he would meet me from work.

On the 2nd July 1960 Pauline and Tom were married at St.Barnabus Church in Walthamstow. She had chosen not to invite Roy and myself in spite of the fact that we had been good friends and had spent quite a bit of time together. Christine and her husband did attend. I went to the Church and saw them married and took some photos afterwards, but I felt really upset at the snub, she was not a friend to me at all and there and then decided that she and Tom would not be invited to mine and Roy's wedding.

I had always been a prolific letter writer and kept in touch with my relatives in Northampton which included my Aunt Rose and Aunt Lil and of course my Nan. I told Aunt Rose that Roy and I were saving to get married the following year and she wrote back and invited us to stay for a week when we had our summer holidays. I spoke to Roy and he said that would be wonderful. We had booked the last two weeks in July so I wrote back to Aunt

176

Rose and asked if it would be ok to come on the last week in July and she quickly wrote back and said that would be fine and to let her know what time we were expecting to arrive and her and Uncle Walt would pick us up in their car.

So that was something to look forward to as it would not cost us very much although we would give Aunt Rose and Uncle Walt some money towards food.

The next few weeks flew by soon it was the end of July. We packed our bags and got a train to Victoria, and then we bought tickets for the Birches coaches which would take us into Rushden. I had already written to Aunt Rose telling her out estimated time of arrival so hopefully she and Uncle Walt would be waiting for us.

The journey took around 2 hours – I still hated the dreaded Birches Coaches but thankfully I had got over my travel sickness. As we alighted from the bus Aunt Rose and Uncle Walt were waiting they put our cases in the boot of their car and off we went to Raunds.

We had a lovely time at Aunt Rose and Uncle Walt's house. They treated us well and Aunt Rose cooked us lovely meals. There was so much on the plate that I couldn't move afterwards. Roy and I would spend the day going out to different places, and one day we even walked all the way to where Nan and Auntie Lil lived and spent the day with them. We were home rather late and Aunt Rose was a bit annoyed because she had made dinner for us and we hadn't told her that we were going to see my Nan. I did apologise to her and said we had decided on the spur of the moment.

Our holiday soon came to an end and Aunt Rose and Uncle Walt drove us back to Rushden bus station where we caught the bus back to Victoria. Then from Victoria we got a train home.

I had a letter from Marion after an absence of some time to say that she had given birth to a little boy in June and had named him Roy. She sent me a photo of him and he looked adorable. She said that she was still living with her parents in Canvey for the time being and asked if Roy and I would like to go for a visit. I wrote back and said I would speak to Roy and then we could make arrangements to come down for a weekend.

So the next fine weekend in the middle of August, Roy and I caught a train to Benfleet then a bus on to the Island. Marion arranged to meet us at the bus stop and we walked to Pine Close where her parents were living. Roy was given the spare room and I shared with Marion and the baby.

The first day Marion put the baby in his pram and we walked down to the seafront and played Bingo and won a set of saucepans. I commented to Roy that they would come in handy for our bottom drawer. We also went into the funfair which brought memories back of the holiday I had spent with Mum and Dad Barry and Veronica. We returned to Marion's parents' house and had some tea and then spent the evening chatting and catching up on all the gossip and news from Walthamstow. Roy got on well with Jack and Millie, Marion's parents whilst Roy sat chatting to Jack Marion and I had a good old chin wag. After all, we had a lot of catching up to do and promised each other that we would keep in touch.

On Sunday it was time for us to leave and as Marion's brother Dave was also going back to Walthamstow we travelled on the train together. It had been a nice change and we had both enjoyed the break. We arrived back at Priory Court late afternoon and I showed mum the saucepans I had won. I had also purchased some bits and pieces to put away for our married life together.

By this time we had had quite a bit saved and we were now talking about when we would get married. I had checked the calendar for 1961 and suggested that perhaps we could get married Easter Saturday, which would fall on 1st April, but first we had to persuade my mum and dad. There was another reason for choosing that date because it would mean if we married before the end of the tax year of 5th April, we would both get tax rebates.

One Saturday afternoon in September when dad was on his own, Roy approached him and taking a big breath said "Would you let me and Maureen get married next April 1st?" I think dad was a bit taken aback but he quickly recovered and said he would talk to my mum

A few days later I asked dad if he had spoken to mum and he replied that as long as we had somewhere to live then yes we could get married.

I was overjoyed and related this message to Roy. Over the next few months we set about arranging our wedding. Dad suggested that we hire the Community Centre for our reception and promised to speak to the Lettings Manager and book it up for us. However before doing so Roy and I had to make an appointment to see the Vicar of the Church in which we were going to get married, which was in my Parish of St. John and we also had to see the Vicar of St. Andrews church which was in Roy's Parish to arrange to have the banns read.

I telephoned the Vicar of St. Johns the Reverend Jones to make an appointment to see him. He asked me what dates we had in mind and I told him 1st April, which of course would be quite busy as it was an Easter Saturday. He checked his diary and said that he did have a space at 4 p.m. so I said that would be fine. He then made an appointment for me and Roy to go and see him. His next question was "How old are you?" I told him that I would be 19 in November. He informed me that I would need written consent from my parents that they agreed to my marriage. I told dad and straight away he wrote a letter which Roy and I took along to the Vicar on the following Wednesday evening.

The Reverend Jones was really nice. He was quite young, I would say in his early 30s and really down to earth. He talked to us at some length about the sanctity of marriage and how important it was to take our vows seriously. He stressed the point that we were both very young and we should be quite certain in our own minds that this is what we wanted to do. I told him that we had been going out with each other for the past 4 years and we were quite certain that we wanted to be together for the rest of our lives. Reverend Jones then asked if we had spoken to the Vicar of Roy's parish and we said that was next on the list but we had wanted to book our wedding with him first.

As we came out of the Vestry I hugged Roy tightly and said I could not believe that at last we were actually getting married. We then made another appointment to see the Vicar of St. Andrews who also gave us a lecture on marriage, and it was arranged to have our Banns called on three successive Sundays in March 1961.

When we got home we told mum and dad that the wedding was all booked for the 01 April at 4 p.m. That weekend as promised dad spoke to the Lettings Manager of the Priory Court Community Centre and booked the hall for us.

Roy and I wrote a list of all the things we had to do and the first on the list was the Caterer. A friend of ours had recommended Halls Caterers in Walthamstow so we arranged to go and see them. The first question we were asked was the date of the wedding and after checking the lady said that it was free. She produced a list of menus from which we chose one at 10s. 6d (52½p) per head which consisted of tomato soup for starters, roast beef with all the trimmings for the main meal and fruit Sundae and ice-cream for dessert. We gave her a rough idea of numbers then paid her a deposit. She asked that we confirm the numbers about a week before the wedding. That was the first item off of our list.

We then began looking at photographers. I had previously used a photographer whose shop was at the end of Palmerston Road. I had gone along to have a portrait photo done which I had given to Roy. The photographer hadn't been established all that long, so I went along to his shop whilst Roy was working and made an appointment for him to bring samples of his work round to mum and dads the next week, as Roy would be on early shift then. The next Saturday soon came around and the photographer was very punctual. I had asked mum and dad to be present as I wanted to include them as much as possible. Roy and I both liked what we saw and as he was young and I think was just starting out in the photography business we thought we would give him the opportunity to take the photos of our wedding.

So that was another item ticked off of our list. The next thing on the list was the flowers. Roy's sister Jean had a friend called Connie who owned a flower shop on the corner of Boundary Road in Leyton which was not far from where Jean lived. Jean had a word with her and I went to see her on my own as this was my domain. I looked through her books; I had a rough idea what I wanted. Connie came up with a few suggestions with the result and we had decided on spring flowers for the bridesmaids and Lemon Tea roses and Lily of the Valley for my bouquet. Connie suggested that I had Victorian posies for the two older girls and baskets for the two smaller bridesmaids, which I thought was a great idea.

Connie asked me about headdresses and I explained that I was going to hire my wedding dress and that of the two older bridesmaids, so she said that she would make the headdresses for the two smaller bridesmaids. She showed me some styles and I chose a coronet of flowers which Connie said she would make to match the flowers in their baskets. I also ordered white carnations for buttonholes. I paid her a deposit and was so excited that all our arrangements were going so well.

Originally I was only going to have 3 bridesmaids, my sister Veronica and Roy's two nieces Colleen – who was almost 15 and Christine who was 4 years old. Then mum asked me if I would also include my Cousin Lynette. She was the daughter of mum's sister Pat and because there were more boys than girls in the family there would not be much opportunity for her to be a bridesmaid. So I said yes I would have her and Auntie Pat kindly offered to pay towards Lynette's bridesmaid's dress which mum said she would make. She also said she would make Christine's dress I had decided to hire the other two together with my wedding dress. I honestly did not think it would be worth buying a wedding dress if I was only going to wear it once. I had decided that I wanted lemon and lavender colour scheme for the bridesmaids.

The next item on the list was the Wedding cake. I knew of a Bakers in the High Street where mum would often go to buy cakes it was called Mays Bakers. So we chose to go there. The lady kindly showed us a brochure of wedding cakes that they produced and we finally chose a 2-tier square cake as we considered it would be easier to cut up. She asked us what decoration we would like on the top, and we chose a small vase of artificial white flowers. The cake cost £6.10s (£6.50p).

Actually there is a funny story attached to this Bakers which I think is worth telling. As I mentioned previously, when we lived in Erskine Road mum would often go in and buy our favourite cakes as a treat which were Lemon Curd tarts. On one occasion she was rather rushed and remembered at the last minute to get the cakes. She waited to be served then when asked what she required she replied "Oh six Lemon TURD cakes please". She quickly corrected herself feeling quite embarrassed but the shop assistant who by this time had got to know mum, fell about laughing.

One Sunday we went to visit my Uncle Bill (mum's brother) and Auntie Eva who lived in Bethnal Green. We often used to go to see him and he would go with us to Petticoat Lane. That in itself was an experience. You could see all the different stalls, with the stallholders shouting their wares. There was a piece of waste ground where one man had set up his stall selling china ware and household items such as saucepans frying pans and so on. He very cleverly took a whole dinner service out and balanced the plates on his wrists and started his spiel "'ere you are ladies and gents, I've got 'ere a lovely bone china dinner service, six side plates and six large dinner plates – this would cost you a fiver in the posh shops, I'm not going to ask a fiver, not four quid, not three quid but two quid for the lot, ave I got any offers?" Of course there was always 'plants' in the crowd who were friends of the stall holder who would put their hands up and before long, other people would buy the china thinking they had a bargain.   On the corner or Petticoat lane was a man selling puppies and kittens, I always thought they looked so sad and if I had had my way I would have banned him from selling them they didn't seem as if they had been well looked after. Of course lots of people did purchase the animals and I hope that they eventually did go to good homes.

By this time I had begun to buy bits and pieces for my bottom drawer, and on this particular Sunday I took the opportunity to look for some sheets and pillowcases. Uncle Bill knew all the right places to go and very soon we had purchased some really nice bed linen. Roy and I told him that we had set the date for our wedding, and to our surprise and delight he offered to get our Wedding Invitations printed. At that time he worked in the printing business so he was able to get a discount. He said he would look out some designs for us to choose from.

We were very lucky in that we managed to get quite a few things cheaper. My Uncle Alf said he would pay for our Wedding Cars and as he was in the car business i.e. fitting tyres and he had a lot of contacts. One of my neighbours worked for the Brewery Tap in St. James Street in Walthamstow and was able to obtain the spirits at cost price. So all in all we saved quite a bit of money.

Mum and dad took the opportunity to visit Auntie Pat and Uncle Wilf who lived on a farm in Cambridgeshire. One of the reasons for the visit was so that mum could take Lynette's measurements for her bridesmaid dress. Mum told Auntie Pat that she would be dressed in Lavender. Lynette was of course very excited as she had never been a bridesmaid before.

Last but not least, we had decided that we would like to go on Honeymoon and there was really only one place where we wanted to go – and that was the Isle of Wight. So I wrote a letter to Mrs. Grey to ask her if we could stay with her from the 2nd April to the 8th April inclusive. I received a letter back saying she would be very happy to have us and she gave us a special rate for the room. I sent off the deposit straight away and that was another item off of our list.

By now I was getting very excited as the months flew by. The two little bridesmaids' dresses were coming on a treat – my mum was so clever. It was time that I sorted out what I was going to wear so I needed to look for my wedding dress. Someone I worked with at LRC suggested that I try Losners in Stamford Hill as being a good place to hire wedding dresses. She said they came highly recommended. So on my 19th birthday, which happened to fall on a Saturday mum, Veronica, Colleen and I got the bus to Stamford Hill. I had been told that the shop was on a corner and the premises were quite large. We eventually found the shop after asking someone in the street.

We opened the door which had a bell on it to announce customers and my first impression of the shop was that it was not very well lit but it had wall to wall dresses, bridesmaids' dresses, evening dresses short and long there was hardly any room to move, and the shop wasn't as large as I had originally envisaged.

There were already a couple of other people waiting so we took a seat, and shortly afterwards an assistant came over to me. I explained that I wanted to hire a wedding dress and two bridesmaids' dresses. She called another lady over and we were taken upstairs to another large room. This time it was wall to wall with wedding dresses.

The lady asked if I had any idea what style I was looking for and I said that I quite liked a crinoline.

She went away and soon came back with 3 wedding dresses over her arm. She then took us into a room on the side which had mirrors all around and which I assumed was the fitting room. She hung two of the dresses up on the rail and gave me the first one to try on. I felt like a fairy princess in each dress I tried, but the last one really took my eye and straight away my mum said "That's the one Maureen that looks lovely on you". I agreed and the assistant also said that she thought that was the dress that suited me. The dress had a white lace bodice and long lace sleeves that came to a point over my hands. The bodice fitted tightly into my waist before flaring out to a wide crinoline skirt. The skirt itself was ruched in tiers falling to the bottom which then draped elegantly to the floor. The neckline was boat-shaped edged with white satin ribbon which went all the way round to the back of the dress into to a V shape ending in a bow with the ends falling down over the back of the dress. There was a wide hooped underskirt beneath the dress just like the crinoline dresses in the 18th century. As mum looked at me she became quite tearful. It must have been hard for her since it was barely 24 years ago when she had got married and now here was her eldest daughter preparing for her wedding.

I was informed by the assistant that the dress would be altered to fit and then it would be dry cleaned ready for collection. She took my measurements and commented on how small my waist was which at time was just 23". She wrote down all the particulars, my name and address and the date of the wedding after she had completed all the details. She then turned her attention to the two bridesmaids. She asked me what colours I wanted and I explained lemon and lavender.

She came back with about 3 dresses in those colours. However this time it was the first dresses that they Veronica and Colleen tried on that I decided were the ones I liked. They were also crinoline style but not as wide as my wedding address. They were the same style, with a boat-shaped neckline, short sleeves and fitted at the waist flaring out into a wide skirt. The assistant produced headdresses to match consisting of a coronet of flowers one each in lemon and lavender. I asked the girls if they were happy with the choice of dresses and they both nodded quite happily. Although previously Colleen had expressed the view that she had worn lemon as a bridesmaid before, and could she have a different colour, but I stuck to my guns and said I thought Lemon suited her better than lavender.

I did ask the assistant about the headdress and veil but she said that would be sorted out when I went for a fitting for the dress and collected it.

I also chose long gloves and satin shoes to go with the bridesmaids dresses, and hired white satin low-heeled shoes to go with the wedding dress – I didn't want to wear my usual high heels as it may have made me taller than Roy. The assistant said that because I was not very tall, they would probably have to insert an extra hoop into the underskirt of the dress to bring it up off the floor a bit more, obviously the reason being that because of the width of the dress, they couldn't make a hem to shorten it.

I paid a deposit and arranged that I would go for a fitting the week prior to the wedding and collect the dresses on the day before, which in this case would be Good Friday. I did mention that I was getting married at Easter but they said that they would be open on Good Friday so that was settled.

I couldn't wait to get home to tell Roy. He was on the late shift finishing at 10 p.m. and on those occasions I would walk down to meet Roy and we would spend an hour at his parents' house before he walked me back to Priory Court.

The following week mum, Veronica and I went along to a big store in Leytonstone called Bearman's where they sold all kinds of haberdashery, dress material and dress patterns. We looked at few patterns for bridesmaids' dresses and I chose one that was really simple. It had short puff sleeves a round neckline, fitted at the waist with a sash and a flared skirt. The dress buttoned up at the back. Mum suggested that a flocked material would look nice in that style. I bought two patterns and then mum and I went to the department where they sold dress material but after some searching could not find what we were looking for. We decided to get on a bus and go to Walthamstow Market. Mum knew of a little shop near the bottom that sold the kind of material we wanted.

We walked into the little shop which was stocked from floor to the ceiling with bolts of material. The assistant came forward and asked if she could help. "Yes please", I said. "We are looking for some flocked material in lemon and lavender and some taffeta in the same colours for the underskirts". "The material is for two bridesmaids dresses" mum said. Straight away the assistant went to the back of the shop and soon came back with two bolts of the flocked material and two bolts of taffeta in the colours I had asked for. Mum produced the patterns and looked to see how much of each material was required and ordered the right amount in both materials which I then paid for. We also bought small some buttons for the dresses which she said she would cover with the same material.

We made our way back home very pleased with our purchases. A few days later mum began cutting out the material from the pattern and started sewing the pieces together on her sewing machine which was in mum and dad's bedroom. She made Christine's dress first as it was the smallest and when it was all pinned up she asked June to bring Christine round for a fitting. After making a few adjustments mum began to sew it all together. Christine's dress was in pale lemon with an underskirt in lemon taffeta. Mum then made a wide sash out of the taffeta material. Christine came round for a final fitting and it was perfect.

Mum then started on Lynette's dress. As she had done with Christine's dress, she cut out the pieces and pinned and tacked them together. Mum and Dad then arranged to go to see Auntie Pat so that Lynette could have a fitting for the dress. Again mum made the adjustments and when she got home again she began sewing it altogether. Mum wrote to Auntie Pat to say the dress was finished and asked if she could possibly bring Lynette up to London for a final fitting. Mum received a reply a few days later to say that Auntie Pat would be coming up in a couple of weeks. When they arrived on the Saturday morning, Lynette tried on her dress and it fitted like a glove.

Roy was getting a bit fed up with doing shift work and his brother-in-law suggested that he tried Hitchmans Dairies in the North Circular Road as they were recruiting. He telephoned the offices and went for an interview which happened to be on his 21st birthday on the 02 January 1961. The Manager who interviewed him said that they only took on people 21 and over and Roy then told him that it was his birthday that day and he was in fact 21. He had to produce his birth Certificate to prove his age. He was offered the job and told he could start the next week.

Hitchmans Dairies had been established many years and produced all the milk that was delivered by Lorries to various depots where the Milkmen would then load up their barrows with their milk to deliver to the customers on their rounds. Hitchmans originally had a farm in Higham Hill some years ago but when old man Hitchman died the farm was sold and the land was used for building houses upon.

Roy started as a 'Spare Man' which meant he could be put in any department to cover anyone who was absent. He soon made a few friends with the other men. They had a large canteen where they would all go for their breaks and midday meals. Also working at the Dairy was Roy's brother-in-law Bill who was married to his sister Jean. It had been Bill who had suggested that Roy apply for a job there. Bill was a driver's mate on the Lorries.

In the meantime, I was getting on really well in my job at the London Rubber Company and after being snubbed by Pauline I had made friends with another girl who at 25 years old was 6 years older than me and her name was Kathy. Like Roy and I she was also planning her wedding to her Fiancé Bill who was a Steward on a passenger liner. She had booked the 25th February when Bill was due home on leave. We would go to lunch together and excitedly discuss the plans for our respective weddings.

Kathy's wedding day soon came around and I had arranged with a couple of the other women to go to the church in Enfield to see her married. I got a bus up to the top of Chingford Mount Road where one of the women lived and it had been arranged between us that her husband would take us in his car.

We arrived at the church. It wasn't a very nice day, very overcast and it was cold, but then you had to expect that sort of weather in February. The bridesmaids were the first to arrive there were three of them, two older girls and a small girl all of whom were dressed in deep red velvet dresses carrying bouquets of white carnations and freesia.

We all filed into the church and took our seats. Bill stood at the Alter with his best man looking very nervous. He was a couple of years younger than Kathy and they had been together for a number of years. Soon the Wedding march struck up and the congregation all stood. We all turned as Kathy began the slow process down the aisle. She looked lovely, dressed in a long slim-line dress fitted at the waist. She wore a glittering tiara on her head

190

from whence fell an elbow-length white veil, and she carried a bouquet of deep red roses to match her bridesmaids' dresses. Kathy at 4ft 11 tall was very petite with long dark hair; she was a very pretty girl and had a lovely personality to match. She reached the Alter and stood by Bill who was quite tall making and in contrast she looked like a dainty doll by his side.

The wedding service was soon over and we followed the wedding party outside where the photos were taken. Kathy had not invited any of her workmates to her wedding as she had planned to have a quiet reception at her parents' home before she and Bill went off for a few days honeymoon. Bill was due back on the Passenger liner for his last trip abroad. They had found a flat in which to settle down and I believe that Bill had planned to leave the sea after one more trip and get a job on shore. Kathy in the meantime returned to work after her short honeymoon.

At the beginning of February, Roy and I began to look around for a flat in which to live. We studied our local Guardian Newspapers every week until one week I found a bedsit to rent which was in Leytonstone. I telephoned the number from the phone box down the road and arranged to go and have a look.

Roy and I got on a bus to Leytonstone and got off at Leyton Midland; we had previously looked at the A to Z and found out where the road was. It was called Forest Drive West and as we got to the bottom of that road, we were surprised at how wide it was and the houses on either side were large with big bay windows. No. 38 was on the right side of the road almost at the top of the road. We knocked on the bit imposing wooden door which was opened by a young lady. She invited us in and we followed her to the room at the back downstairs. She explained that the house was owned jointly by her and her sister and they each had half of the house where they lived with their respective families. The young Lady's name was Rose and her husband Terry and she introduced us to her mother who also lived with them and she said they had a little girl who was 3 years old.

She took us upstairs which was on the side of the house that she owned, and showed us to a large room. Inside was a settee which doubled as a put-u-up. There was an oven in the corner, a sink and over on the other side a dresser with a cupboard above it, it had a drop-down section with cupboards beneath it. There was also an electric fire. The rent was £2.10s (£2.50p) per week. She explained that we would share the bathroom and toilet which was outside on the landing. She left us to discuss it and said when we were ready she would be downstairs.

I looked at Roy and said "What do you think?" Roy looked around and said "Well it would do us for now until we can find something better; at least we will have somewhere to go once we are married". So we decided to take it. We went downstairs and politely knocked on the door to Rose's sitting room and said we would take the room. We paid her a months' rent in advance and told her that we would be moving in a few days before our wedding. She said that was fine.

We then went home quite happy that we had found somewhere. It was not as we had planned but it was a start and as time was getting short and it was only a few weeks away to the wedding it was one worry out of the way.

When I told mum that we had found a bedsit, she wasn't very impressed and said that we should have waited and got a flat, but I explained to her that although we had both been looking for weeks there hadn't been anything that we could afford, so at least we had somewhere to go when we did get married, and once we were settled we could start saving again and then look for something better.

Over the next few weeks we began moving some of our stuff that we had either bought or which had been bought for us as engagement presents. The room which had looked quite austere and cold began to look quite homely.

On the first Saturday in March Roy and I went to the High Street to purchase my wedding ring. Roy was adamant that he didn't want a separate wedding ring but would keep his engagement ring which would double as his wedding ring. We looked in all the jewellers' windows and finally we saw the ring I liked in Hinds the Jewellers. We went into the shop and asked to see the tray of Wedding Rings. I chose a plain 22 carat gold ring in a barrel shape approximately $1/8^{th}$ inch wide. I tried it on and placed my engagement ring on top of it. They went well together and it was a perfect fit so it didn't need any alteration at all. Roy said to the assistant "We'll have this one please". The ring was placed into a nice velvet box and we received a free gift of a silver cake server. The ring was £7.10s (£7.50p) which was quite a lot of money in those days considering that I only earned £6.12s (£6.52½p in today's money) per week.

I couldn't wait to show the ring to mum and dad, and mum said that it was a good choice. She told me that when she and dad were getting married her mother had gone with them and had insisted on the ring being weighed to ascertain its penny weight to make sure that they got a bargain. Apparently that was what they did in those days. Mum's ring was also 22 carat plain gold but not as wide as the one Roy had just bought for me.

On the Friday before the wedding mum, Colleen, Veronica and I went to Losners for a final fitting of our dresses. They had done a good job and all the dresses fitted us perfectly. The lady then said I had to choose a headdress and she brought out a few for me to try. I chose one made of crystals in a tiara shape. The assistant asked what type of veil I wanted and I said an elbow length. I paid the balance of the fee and arranged to collect all the dresses the following Friday.

Finally on the Thursday before the wedding, we managed to get a mattress delivered to the bedsit which we had bought to put on the Settee. We had looked at it and to be honest it hadn't looked very comfortable. The mattress fitted on ok and it folded up inside the settee without any problems. We spent one last night of freedom together before making our way home. Roy had planned to have his stag night in the Prince public house which was in the same road as Bowater's where had had worked. He had invited some of his friends he had worked with as well as some new friends from Hitchmans Dairies. I had arranged to go out with 2 or 3 friends to the Standard Pub opposite Blackhorse Road Station.

Each month the London Rubber Company produced a Staff magazine so the person who did the editing heard about my wedding and asked me to write details down of my dress and bridesmaids etc., so that it would appear in the next month's edition. So I wrote all the details down and handed it in to the office when I went in the next day.

At last the week of the wedding arrived and I only had to work four days as did everyone else because of the Easter holiday. My last day was Thursday and I got ready for work feeling quite nervous and apprehensive. I had an idea that my colleagues were planning something as normally when a staff member was getting married they did a presentation. I met a couple of the girls on the bus going to work and they walked along with me and I thought at the time that they were walking rather slowly, but I was anxious to get into work so I began to walk a bit faster.

We walked into the reception and said good morning to the Receptionist then we clocked in. I went through the double doors that led to the office and stopped as I looked down towards where I usually sat and the whole of my desk and been transformed with banners and balloons. The girls were all gathered around waiting for me to come in. They told me afterwards that they had all got in to work an hour early so they could decorate my desk.

After I had hung up my coat I walked into the Advertising department where I worked. There was a pile of presents on my desk all wrapped in pretty wedding paper as well as a pile of envelopes containing cards. I sat down and started with the cards which were from all the various people who worked in the other departments. I then unwrapped the presents. I was quite overwhelmed with the generosity of all my work mates. Amongst the presents I received was a tea service, a set of teaspoons, tea towels, a bale of hand and bath towels and flannels. There were lots of other smaller presents as well.

Then our Manager Mr. Ross-Turner came out of his office carrying a big parcel "Here you are Miss Penn (he was always very formal and never addressed me by my first name) congratulations on your forthcoming marriage and I hope you and your fiancé will be very happy together". Placing the huge parcel in my arms I laid it on the desk in front of me and began carefully taking the paper from it. Inside was a beautiful Lavender Witney blanket edged in satin? "Oh it's lovely; it's just what I wanted, thank you all so much". Mr.Ross-Turner said it was from the entire department and the Managers. I turned to Dora who was one of my colleagues and asked how she knew what colour I liked. She said that they had been a bit crafty in getting me to talk about colour schemes I would like when we eventually got a bigger place to live.

I had also mentioned that during the time Roy had been in Wales I had sent away for a rug-making set this consisted of the hessian backing which had a pattern printed onto it. Included in the pack was the wool in the colours I had specified which in this case were lavender and grey; there were hooks used for weaving the wool into the backing and of course the pattern which we had to follow. I had started it off and when Roy was home he would help me with it. We had finally finished it and were pleased with the result. The rug was approximately 4ft long by 3ft wide with a grey background with Lavender flowers woven in the corners of the rug. So of course the girls had gleaned all this information from me.

Pretty soon it was time for our tea break. We had two ladies who came round with a trolley on which was a tea urn cups and saucers, sandwiches and rolls which we bought if we were hungry. We soon heard the rumble of the tea trolley wheels as they came through the double doors at the end of the office. The canteen itself was situated at the far end of the factory so they had to wheel their tea trolley through the factory to the office.

The tea ladies were so nice. There was Elsie who was I suppose in her late fifties, she was around 5ft tall with short blond hair and to keep her hair tidy and obviously for health reasons she wore a white cap with a hairnet attached. She was always immaculately dressed in a white overall and tucked in the pocket was a lace handkerchief. She wore discreet makeup and there was a wisp of perfume as she walked by.

Her companion was the complete opposite. Her name was Lilly, she was tall and thin with dark hair. She also wore a white overall and a cap and hairnet on her head.

We always had a laugh with the pair of them and sometimes Mr.Ross-Turner would come out of his office and tell us to keep the noise down. Elsie and Lilly came over to me and handed to me a large envelope and when I opened it there was a wedding card inside which had been signed by all the Canteen Staff and I was quite overwhelmed with their generosity. They both congratulated me before going back to the tea trolley to serve the staff their morning tea. Mr.Ross-Turner was always served his first. When Elsie brought my tea over to me I asked her if she had ordered the cakes for that afternoon that I had asked for and she confirmed that she had.

The day went quite swiftly and I was so excited that I found it hard to settle down to do any work. At 2.30 Elsie and Lilly came round with the afternoon tea and they had brought boxes of fancy cakes which I had paid for to give out to the staff. Mr.Ross-Turner then came out of his office and called me in. I wondered what he was going to say and he asked me to sit down. "Right Miss Penn, I can see that you are going to have some difficulty in getting all those presents home so I have arranged for one of the lads to take you home in the one of the company cars and you can leave an hour early as it is a special occasion. I hope you have a lovely day on Saturday and that the sun shines on you". I thanked him profusely, he was a nice man and I had always got on well with him. "Right then we will see you back in a week's time".

The women in my department helped me pack all the presents together and at 4 p.m. the driver came up to the office and helped me take all the presents out and load them into the company car which he had parked at the front of the building. I said my goodbyes and was quite tearful. Then I was driven home. When we arrived he helped me put all the presents in the lift and I thanked him and he left. I managed to get up to our flat on the third floor and got all the presents out and knocked on the door so that mum and dad could help me with them. "Blimey what have you got there?" dad said as he helped carry them all in. "They are all presents from the people in work – aren't I lucky". For the time being we put them all in the bedroom that I shared with Veronica

I was up early the next day as it was Good Friday and we were collecting the dresses from Losners. Once again our neighbour Bob had kindly offered to take us there and bring us back home.

We arrived about mid-morning and left Bob to find somewhere to park. We entered the shop and I gave my name and then we were taken upstairs. The dresses were already covered in polythene dress bags ready for our collection. The assistant showed me my headdress on which they had sewn a veil. I tried it on and mum said it did look nice. The assistant carefully packed this into a box and then mum and I took all the dresses downstairs. The Assistant told me that they had to be returned on Sunday.

Mum said she was sure that one of our relatives would be happy to take the dresses back for us as it was impossible for Roy and me to do so as we were going on honeymoon the day after the wedding. We made a joint decision to enjoy all of our wedding day including the evening even though traditionally a lot of newly married couples left their reception to go on honeymoon, after all there would be a lot of relations on my side of the family who I didn't get to see that often.

We arrived back home and Bob helped us carefully carry the dresses upstairs where I hung them on the outside of the wardrobe. I thanked Bob for all his help and said that I would see him and his family at the evening reception the next day. After we had our tea I got ready to go out to meet my friends for my Hen night whilst mum went over to Priory Court for her usual Bingo night. I walked down to the Standard Public House and as I was a bit nervous about going into a pub on my own I waited outside. I waited, and waited, but no-one turned up. I felt quite tearful and let down so I decided to go back home and I went to the Community Centre and made my way to the table where mum was sitting with her friends. She was surprised to see me and I told her what had occurred. "Never mind love, sit down with us and play bingo to take your mind off of it, they can't be very nice friends if they let you down". Halfway through the evening they had a break, and the Bingo Caller – his name was Harry Pattle who was the Chairman of the Community Centre Committee, announced to everyone that I was getting married the next day. Everybody clapped and wished me every happiness; I went quite red and felt little bit embarrassed.

The evening had ended better than I had thought and mum and I made our way back home. We had a cup of hot chocolate before I retired for the night. I lay awake for quite a time realising that this would be the last night I would spend in my single bed, and in the bedroom I shared with my sister Veronica. I looked at my wedding dress hanging outside the wardrobe and felt very excited.

The day of our wedding dawned but to my great disappointment it had been raining and it was still drizzling. I had my breakfast then got ready to go to the hairdressers. Luckily the rain had stopped although I did take my umbrella as a precaution.

My hairdresser Betty greeted me and wished me all the best and said if she could get away, she would pop round before I was ready to go to the church and come up and put my veil on for me and make sure it was pinned securely. I thanked her and left. It was still quite dull out but the rain had stopped.

I quickly had a bite to eat and then had to go to the Walthamstow Market to get one or two bits and pieces including a wedding present for my husband-to-be. I finally chose a pair of cufflinks and a tie pin to match.

Soon it was time to start getting ready but first mum and I went to the Community Centre to take the Wedding cake over. The caterers were already there getting the tables ready so we left the cake with them.

Colleen was late getting round to my flat and I was a bit annoyed over this. June had already brought Christine over and my Aunt Pat and Uncle Wilf had arrived with Lynette and her brother Noel. The bridesmaids got ready first and they went into the lounge whilst I went into my mum and dad's bedroom to change into my wedding dress.

I had told mum that Betty was hoping to come over and help me secure my veil but time was getting on so I sat at my mum's dressing table and put on a little bit of makeup – I never used to wear very much as luckily I had good skin, and just put on a touch of lipstick. I fastened a crucifix around my neck that my mum had given me. Finally I said to mum that we couldn't wait any longer for Betty so mum and my Aunt Hetty put my veil on. Mum had gone to the chemist shop downstairs to buy some white hair clips, so between them they managed to put my veil on for me, although it didn't feel very secure. Aunt Rose had brought her own wedding veil with her as she was willing to lend it to me and although it was a beautiful long veil made of lace, I didn't think that it would go with my crinoline dress and in any case the people at Losners had already attached my headdress to the veil that I had chosen to wear.

Mum had looked out of the window and spotted Betty's car but she didn't come up so I guess she thought it was a bit late and hopefully she would be in the church to see me get married.

The cars arrived and the bridesmaids went in the first car with mum. Before leaving for the church my Nanny Penn had given me a sixpence and told me to put it in my shoe for luck. I still have that sixpence which is sellotaped on the front inside cover of a separate photo album which I put together with all the photos I collected that had been taken by my friends and relatives. These also included coloured photos taken by Uncle Bill which were something new in photography.

My Aunts and Uncles made their own way in their vehicles, and so it was just my dad and me. I began to feel terribly nervous. It was time to go; the first problem we encountered was that I couldn't go down in the lift, firstly because my dress was too wide, and even if it hadn't been the lift was quite dirty. So dad and I had to go down 6 flights of stairs. My friends Brenda and Angela came out from across the way and wished me luck. Brenda even offered to help me down the stairs but dad said thank you but that we could manage. So with dad carrying my bouquet and me holding up my dress we made our slow way down the stairs, on the way doors opened and my neighbours were all out on their balconies or standing downstairs in the street and some of them shouted out their good wishes as I walked towards the wedding car.

I walked across the front of our block into the waiting wedding car and settled in. I held dad's hand and for the first time I felt close to him. As we arrived at the church we saw a big crowd of people who were obviously nothing to do with our wedding. As it was Easter the church had been busy and somewhere along the line one bride had arrived late which had pushed all the other weddings behind. Our driver had no option but to drive around the block and as we drove down St. John's Road I spotted Roy outside with his Best man who was his brother Jimmy. Jimmy quickly turned Roy around so that he wouldn't see me.

Finally at 4.15 p.m. a quarter of an hour late, we pulled up outside the entrance to the church in St. John's Road. Regrettably the front of the church had been damaged during the war and the Church was still trying to get funding to rebuild it, so that meant I had to enter by the side door, and walk the whole length of the church to the bottom of the aisle before commencing my journey up the central aisle.

As we came into the Church mum was sitting in the front with my brother Barry and she got up and adjusted my veil and straightened the tiara. Dad and I made our progress down the side aisle and reached the bottom. Whether it was dad being over anxious or me, I can't remember, but we began walking up the centre aisle before the vicar had had time to meet us. Reverend Jones quickly made his way down and we followed him up the aisle, everyone's eyes was upon us and I began to feel quite nervous but happy and I felt like a princess in my wedding dress. As I reached the alter Roy was standing there and he whispered "Oh you look beautiful" That made my day because although people had said I looked lovely to actually hear my Bridegroom say it made me feel 10 feet tall.

The ceremony began and Roy placed the ring upon the third finger of my left hand, his hands felt clammy and he was shaking with nerves. I looked down at the shiny gold band on my left hand and could not take it all in. We sang the hymns that Roy and I had chosen and then when we were man and wife, together with our parents and the bridesmaids the Vicar led us into the Vestry where Roy and I signed the Register – that was the last time I would ever sign my single name of 'Penn'. The photographer was there taking photos. I had been a bit disappointed because I had arranged that the photographer would come to mum and dad's flat to take photos of me and the bridesmaids. I did ask him about that, and he apologised saying that he had had another wedding which unfortunately had run on late and so it had delayed him getting to Mum and Dad's flat before the wedding.

The organ stuck up the Wedding march and I still go cold every time I hear this played. Roy and I led the way down the aisle, we reached the bottom and we had our first disagreement of our married life when Roy said we had to turn left and I thought the Vicar had told us to turn right, but Roy was correct, as the door on the left led out to the church grounds where we were to have our photographs taken.

It was over so quickly I felt like I was floating on air and not really taking everything in. After the photos had been taken Roy and I made our way to the Wedding car for one more photo as we posed by the car then we got in to go to the reception. As we drove off Roy put his arm round me and said "Hello Mrs. Shanks".

During the late 50s and early 60s fashion trends had changed and young men were now wearing 'Teddy Boy' suits. The name had derived from the Edwardian era when the males wore long jackets almost to the knee with tight trousers. As they say, *'What goes around comes around'.* Indeed my brother-in-law David – Roy's youngest brother - was no exception and followed the fashion for Teddy boy outfits. To go with the ensemble the hair had to be collar length and greased and swept back to form a 'V' at the back commonly known as a 'DA short for 'Ducks Arse' because of the way the hair overlapped at the bottom. Then the front of the hair would be rolled forward on to the forehead resembling a kind of elephants' trunk.

David arrived at our wedding in full 'Teddy Boy' regalia wearing navy blue jacket down to his knees, tight 'drainpipe' trousers and a navy waistcoat. He wore a white shirt and a bootlace tie. His shoes were 'winkle 'pickers' so called because the toes came to a ridiculous point at the end.

On the other hand, my brother Barry rode a Vespa Scooter so he was considered a 'Mod' rivalry between so-called Teddy Boys and Mods was well documented. However Barry was not a 'Mod' in the true sense of the word in that he didn't attend Scooter rallies, but he did wear the uniform of a Parka Jacket and tied to his aerial on the back of his scooter was an imitation fox tail. He expressed a desire to come to our wedding on his scooter and wearing his Parka Jacket but I put my foot down in that respect. However I had no control over David's apparel.

After the ceremony my new husband and I arrived in Priory Court within about 10 minutes as it was only a short distance from the church. The driver got out and opened the door, Roy got out first and then turned to help me and as I stepped out of the car I felt the underskirt of my dress come adrift. Holding both dress and underskirt up I hurried into the Hall. One of the waitresses was there to greet us and I said that I thought my underskirt was coming undone so she quickly ushered me into the Ladies toilets. Luckily she had some safety pins on her and as suspected the Hook and Eye on the waistband had come adrift. She quickly pinned the waistband together and I went in to the hall to join Roy who was waiting to greet our guests and who were fast arriving after us. I told him what had happened and he smiled. That was something to remember in years to come. As our guests arrived they were served with drinks as they came in.

Very soon it was time to be seated. The Master of Ceremonies told Roy and me to wait outside whilst our guests found their seats. Then in a loud voice he announced "may I present your Bride and Bridegroom Mr and Mrs. Shanks", and then we walked in to applause and sat at the head of the table with our parents and bridesmaids.

The meal was excellent and we enjoyed it very much. Then we had the cake-cutting ceremony and our photographer was there to record this moment. As soon as he had taken the photographs he left as he had to develop the photos and bring them back later that evening so our guests could look at them and choose whether or not they wished to buy any of them.

The Band arrived and set up their instruments and soon the evening guests were arriving. Unfortunately Marion was unable to come to the wedding but Jack; her father did make it so I was rather pleased to see him. He congratulated Roy and me on our marriage and commented on how nice I looked in my wedding dress.

I kept my wedding dress on for the most of the evening, before going back to mum and dad's flat to change into another outfit at around 9 o'clock. Looking back now, I wish I had kept the dress on right until the end of the evening; at least I would have got my money's worth out of wearing the dress. Still it is easy to look back in hindsight. As I was changing mum came and said the photographer had arrived.

Everyone was crowding around the table that had been set up to display the photos and he took many orders. He said he would come round with a sample album for us when we returned from Honeymoon. The photos had come out quite well and Roy and I were pleased. A lot of our guests gave the photographer their orders and he took down names and addresses and said that the photos would be with them in a few weeks.

All too soon our reception came to an end and the band was playing the last waltz. I had mixed feelings of sadness to be leaving my childhood behind, but elation and excitement to be starting a whole new life with the man I loved.

Our guests began leaving for home and my Aunts and Uncles who had arrived from Northampton were booked in at a local hotel but a couple of them were staying with mum and dad. Between us we took our wedding presents and the Wedding cake over to mum and dad's flat where we would arrange to take them to our Bedsit when we returned from honeymoon the following week. Mum had asked me where we were spending our Wedding night and I told her that we intended to go to the bedsit in Leytonstone. She asked why we couldn't stay with them for the night and then they could all see us off the next day. I said no, Roy and I wanted to spend some time on our own after all the excitement of the wedding. I think in a way she was realizing that her little girl was now married and she was trying to keep me with her just a bit longer.

So we said our goodbyes and as usual Bob took us home to our little Bedsit in Leytonstone. He said he and his family had very much enjoyed the evening and thanked Roy and I for inviting them, but we both said that it was us that should be thanking him for running us about in his car. He said that when we returned from honeymoon he would be there to take all our presents home for us.

It felt strange getting undressed and getting into bed with Roy, we were so tired that we just fell asleep. We were up bright and early the next morning. We just had a piece of toast and a cup of tea then gathering our suitcases which we had packed before the wedding, we made our way to the Leyton Midland Station at the bottom of the road. We were soon on our way to Waterloo where we would pick up the train to take us to Portsmouth and from there we would get on the passenger ferry to the Isle of Wight.

I had dressed in my going away outfit of a Navy Blue and White dress with a fitted bolero to match. Over my dress I wore pale blue coat, blue gloves and to finish off the ensemble I wore a blue feathered hat and white high heels. Roy said that I looked really nice and commented again on how lovely I had looked in my wedding dress.

The journey went smoothly and we were soon on the Ferry making our way to the Isle of Wight. I needed the toilet and in those days you had to pay a penny to use the toilet and as I didn't have one I asked my new husband if he could give me a penny. As he fished in his pocket to find the coin a load of confetti fell out. There we were trying to pretend we were a long married couple when that gave us away and other passengers looked at us and smiled.

The weather wasn't very kind to us it had begun to rain. We alighted from the Ferry and caught the train from Cowes to Sandown Station where we found the bus that would take us to Sandown Seafront. From there we had a bit of a walk before reaching Mrs. Grey's boarding house.

She greeted us and congratulated us on our marriage and asked us all about the day. She had dinner all ready for us which we were very grateful for as we hadn't really had very much to eat since leaving that morning.

The next few days were wonderful. Even though we had visited the Island 2 years before when we had come on holiday with Maisie, Bert and Colleen it was nice re-discovering all the sights again.

It was still overcast and at times we had rain. We would spend our evenings either sitting in Mrs. Grey's parlour or visiting the local public house which had just been built at the far end of Sandown and was named 'The Yaverland'. The weather hadn't let up at all so it made it difficult getting around and seeing the sights as we had to rely on the buses, so I suggested that maybe we could book up a coach tour. We walked into Sandown High Street where we knew there was a shop where they dealt with coach tours around the Island. We booked up for one which travelled over the island and included a visit to Osborne House which was built by Queen Victoria's husband Prince Albert.

The next day was a Wednesday, we had breakfast at Mrs. Grey's and told her that we were going on a coach tour and would you believe it the sun came out. In fact that Wednesday was the hottest day of the week. We didn't have to wear coats for the first time that week and it was very enjoyable. As we both liked history it was interesting looking around the house and the gardens. There were even little wheelbarrows and gardening implements which had been made especially for the Queen and Prince Albert's many children.

The remainder of the week flew by and we were soon packing to return home. Before we left on the Saturday morning Mrs. Grey gave us a small present of an ashtray which I thought was really nice of her. "Don't forget you are always welcome and if all goes well, I hope to see you back here next year" Mrs. Grey said as she gave us both a hug.

We arrived home in the early afternoon and made our weary way back to our bedsit. "I think we had better go and do some shopping and get something in for dinner tomorrow" I said. So leaving our cases in the room we took some shopping bags and together we walked along Leytonstone High Street and bought a chicken for the Sunday dinner and some vegetables. We also purchased bread and butter and fillings for the week. Although having no refrigerator I was going to have to do shopping each day.

We had our first night back in our bedsit and I unpacked our clothes and put them in the washing basket which I intended to take to the Launderette in the High Road the next day.

We were up bright and early and Roy came with me to the Launderette and together we found out how to use the washing machines – I had never experienced this before because my mother now had a twin tub washing machine and I had never had reason to use it. However it was quite simple so we got the hang of it and then used the driers to dry the clothes off. When we got back I prepared the chicken and put it in the oven. That was another new experience as the oven was electric and I had been used to gas at my parents' house.

After about a couple of hours I thought that the chicken was taking a long time to cook so I opened the oven and there was no heat at all and the chicken was as raw as when I had put it in the oven a couple of hours earlier. So I went downstairs to Rose and Terry's and knocked on the door and asked if Terry could have a look at the oven for me. I explained that I had tried to cook the chicken but I didn't think the oven was working. So Rose kindly offered to cook it for me. In the meantime, Terry went upstairs and had a look and discovered that a fuse had gone which he mended and apologised. Roy and I ended up having spam, mashed potatoes and peas, but at least we did get to eat a meal. We saved the chicken that Rose had kindly cooked for us for the next day's dinner.

We were both due back to work the next day. Roy had bought himself a bicycle as he had to start work at 6 a.m. but he finished early. I had previously found out which buses went where so I made sure I left sufficient time to get the bus and arrive at work time.

I was quite busy that morning and at break time all women I worked with wanted to know all about the wedding and the honeymoon. Time went quickly and it was time to go home. The journey home took an hour and I was quite tired by the time I had got off the bus and walked the length of the road to our bedsit. I had done a bit of shopping in my lunch hour so when I got in Roy and I prepared the dinner between us and sat down and ate the chicken from the day before which was really tasty.

Roy said we should go and see our parents as we had not seen them since the wedding so we decided to go the next evening. We arranged that I would get off the bus at the Crooked Billet and Roy would meet me and we would both walk round first of all to see his Mum and Dad and then walk round to see mine.

So the next evening as planned I caught the bus down to the Crooked Billet and as I alighted from the bus Roy was there waiting; together we walked along Billet Road and then to his parents' house in Priors Croft. They were so pleased to see us and we spent an hour with them before walking down the road and turning right into Priory Court.

Mum and Dad were really surprised to see us. There was no way we could let them know we would be coming around as they didn't possess a telephone at that time.

Mum said that she had spoken to Bob upstairs and who had very kindly taken us home on our Wedding night and he had offered to take our Wedding presents to our bedsit for us. So I went upstairs and knocked on his door and he said that when we were ready to leave he would load up his car and take us home. I thanked him. I returned to Mum and Dad's flat and I asked mum to get our Wedding Cake so that I could cut some and give to their neighbour Bob and his wife. Mum brought the cake out still in its box and then told me that she had taken the liberty of cutting some of it up and taking it in to give to her work mates in the Co-op shop where she worked in Priory Court. I was quite annoyed at this and said that she had no right to do that to which she replied that I was being mean and surely I didn't begrudge a bit of cake to her friends. At this juncture Dad intervened and agreed with me, he said that Mum should have asked first and not just taken the cake. So that was my first argument with my mum. We smoothed things over afterwards and I think she got the message. It wasn't that I begrudged her friends having some cake, but it was the fact that she hadn't asked.

Mum had told me that one of my Uncles had taken all the dresses back for me on the Sunday so I didn't have to worry and I promised to write a letter to them thanking them.

There was a knock on the door and Bob stood on the doorstep and dad invited him in. I gave him some wedding cake for him and his family and thanked him very much for all he had done taking us to collect the dresses and also for taking our wedding presents home. He replied "Well Maureen that's what neighbours are for".

The first week back to work went swiftly and on the way in to work on Friday of that first week I bought the local Guardian. Our photographer had promised to put a photo and a report on the family page for us. I skipped through the paper until I came to the 'Births, Deaths and Marriage page, and there in pride of place was a photo of

Roy and me cutting our cake with a nice report beneath the photo. Of course all my workmates commented on how nice I looked.

So one chapter of my life had ended and another was about to begin as **Mrs. Maureen Shanks.**

Above: Auntie Rose preparing to do s some washing July 1960
Roy and Maureen at Uncle Walt's &Auntie Rose's house

Pauline & Tom's Wedding 02.07.1960

Above: Bill and Kathy just married.

*Below: Bill and Kathy with their bridesmaids
25 February 1961*

Roy and Maureen's wedding day 01 April 1961

*Maureen and Roy share a toast at their reception
In Priory Court Community Centre. 1961*

Our Wedding day with our bridesmaids and Best Man Jimmy.

219

ABOUT THE AUTHOR

Maureen was born in Thorpe Coombe Maternity Hospital in 1941 and has spent all her life in Walthamstow. She met her husband when she was 15 years old and married at the age of 19. She has two sons, one grandson and a grown-up step-granddaughter.

She worked for most of her married life as a Personal Assistant/Secretary and Legal Secretary. After she retired she set up her own Secretarial business and works part-time for a local Solicitor.

Maureen lives with her husband Roy and has an active life enjoying gardening, solving crossword puzzles and is also a keen golfer and can often be found on the golf course with both of her sons and her grandson who is a budding 'Tiger Woods'. She began writing some years ago beginning with short stories for her grandson Daniel and has now produced her autobiography mainly because Daniel likes to hear stories of when she was a little girl. She very much hopes that the book-lovers will enjoy reading her story as much as she enjoyed writing it.